English / Chinese
英文 / 中文

THE OXFORD
Picture
Dictionary

NORMA SHAPIRO AND JAYME ADELSON-GOLDSTEIN

Translated by Techno-Graphics & Translations, Inc.

Oxford University Press

Oxford University Press
198 Madison Avenue, New York, NY 10016 USA
Great Clarendon Street, Oxford OX2 6DP England

Oxford New York
Auckland Bangkok Buenos Aires Cape Town Chennai
Dar es Salaam Delhi Hong Kong Istanbul Karachi Kolkata
Kuala Lumpur Madrid Melbourne Mexico City Mumbai
Nairobi São Paulo Shanghai Taipei Tokyo Toronto

OXFORD is a trademark of Oxford Unviersity Press.

Library of Congress Cataloging-in Publication Data

Shapiro, Norma.
     The Oxford picture dictionary, English-Chinese/
Norma Shapiro and Jayme Adelson-Goldstein; translation
by Techno-Graphics and Translations, Inc.
          p.   cm.
     Includes bibliographical references and index.
     ISBN 0-19-435189-0
     1. English language—Dictionaries—Chinese.
     2. Picture dictionaries, English.
I. Adelson-Goldstein, Jayme.
PL1455.S415 1998   97-50610
423'.951—dc21   CIP

No unauthorized photocopying.

Translation reviewed by Patrick Yuennong Ng and
Cambridge Translation resources
Editorial Manager: Susan Lanzano
Art Director: Lynn Luchetti
Senior Editor: Eliza Jensen
Senior Designer: Susan P. Brorein
Senior Production Editor: Pat P O'Neill
Art Buyer: Tracy A. Hammond
Production Services by: Techno-Graphics and Translations, Inc.
Pronunciation Editor: Sharon Goldstein
Cover design by Silver Editions

Printing (last digit): 10 9

Printed in China

Illustrations by: David Aikins, Doug Archer, Craig Attebery,
Garin Baker, Sally Bensusen, Eliot Bergman, Mark Bischel, Dan
Brown / Artworks NY, Roy Douglas Buchman, George Burgos /
Larry Dodge, Rob Burman, Carl Cassler, Mary Chandler, Robert
Crawford, Jim DeLapine, Judy Francis, Graphic Chart and Map
Co., Dale Gustafson, Biruta Akerbergs Hansen, Marcia
Hartsock, C.M.I., David Hildebrand, The Ivy League of Artists,
Inc. / Judy Degraffenreid, The Ivy League of Artists, Inc. / Tom
Powers, The Ivy League of Artists, Inc. / John Rice, Pam
Johnson, Ed Kurtzman, Narda Lebo, Scott A. MacNeill /
MACNEILL & MACINTOSH, Andy Lendway / Deborah Wolfe
Ltd., Jeffrey Mangiat, Suzanne Mogensen, Mohammad
Mansoor, Tom Newsom, Melodye Benson Rosales, Stacey
Schuett, Rob Schuster, James Seward, Larry Taugher, Bill
Thomson, Anna Veltfort, Nina Wallace, Wendy Wassink-
Ackison, Michael Wepplo, Don Wieland
Thanks to Mike Mikos for his preliminary architectural sketches
of several pieces.

References
Boyer, Paul S., Clifford E. Clark, Jr., Joseph F. Kett, Thomas L.
Purvis, Harvard Sitkoff, Nancy Woloch *The Enduring Vision: A
History of the American People*, Lexington, Massachusetts:
D.C. Heath and Co., 1990.

Grun, Bernard, *The Timetables of History: A Horizontal Linkage
of People and Events,* (based on Werner Stein's Kulturfahrplan)
New York: A Touchstone Book, Simon and Schuster, 1946,
1963, 1975, 1979.

Statistical Abstract of the United States: 1996, 116th Edition,
Washington, DC: US Bureau of the Census, 1996.

The World Book Encyclopedia, Chicago: World Book Inc., a
Scott Fetzer Co., 1988 Edition.

Toff, Nancy, Editor-in-Chief, *The People of North America*
(Series), New York: Chelsea House Publishers, Main Line
Books, 1988.

Trager, James, *The People's Chronology, A Year-by-Year Record
of Human Events from Prehistory to the Present,* New York:
Henry Holt Reference Book, 1992.

Acknowledgments

The publisher and authors would like to thank the following people for reviewing the manuscript and/or participating in focus groups as the book was being developed:

Ana Maria Aguilera, Lubie Alatriste, Ann Albarelli, Margaret Albers, Sherry Allen, Fiona Armstrong, Ted Auerbach, Steve Austen, Jean Barlow, Sally Bates, Sharon Batson, Myra Baum, Mary Beauparlant, Gretchen Bitterlin, Margrajean Bonilla, Mike Bostwick, Shirley Brod, Lihn Brown, Trish Brys-Overeem, Lynn Bundy, Chris Bunn, Carol Carvel, Leslie Crucil, Jill DeLa Llata, Robert Denheim, Joshua Denk, Kay Devonshire, Thomas Dougherty, Gudrun Draper, Sara Eisen, Lynda Elkins, Ed Ende, Michele Epstein, Beth Fatemi, Andra R. Fawcett, Alice Fiedler, Harriet Fisher, James Fitzgerald, Mary Fitzsimmons, Scott Ford, Barbara Gaines, Elizabeth Garcia Grenados, Maria T. Gerdes, Penny Giacalone, Elliott Glazer, Jill Gluck de la Llata, Javier Gomez, Pura Gonzales, Carole Goodman, Joyce Grabowski, Maggie Grennan, Joanie Griffin, Sally Hansen, Fotini Haritos, Alice Hartley, Fernando Herrera, Ann Hillborn, Mary Hopkins, Lori Howard, Leann Howard, Pamela Howard, Rebecca Hubner, Jan Jarrell, Vicki Johnson, Michele Kagan, Nanette Kafka, Gena Katsaros, Evelyn Kay, Greg Keech, Cliff Ker, Gwen Kerner-Mayer, Marilou Kessler, Patty King, Linda Kiperman, Joyce Klapp, Susan Knutson, Sandy Kobrine, Marinna Kolaitis, Donna Korol, Lorraine Krampe, Karen Kuser, Andrea Lang, Nancy Lebow, Tay Lesley, Gale Lichter, Sandie Linn, Rosario Lorenzano, Louise Louie, Cheryl Lucas, Ronna Magy, Juanita Maltese, Mary Marquardsen, Carmen Marques Rivera, Susan McDowell, Alma McGee, Jerry McLeroy, Kevin McLure, Joan Meier, Patsy Mills, Judy Montague, Vicki Moore, Eneida Morales, Glenn Nadelbach, Elizabeth Neblett, Kathleen Newton, Yvonne Nishio, Afra Nobay, Rosa Elena Ochoa, Jean Owensby, Jim Park, John Perkins, Jane Pers, Laura Peskin, Maria Pick, Percy Pleasant, Selma Porter, Kathy Quinones, Susan Ritter, Martha Robledo, Maureen Rooney, Jean Rose, David Ross, Julietta Ruppert, Lorraine Ruston, Susan Ryan, Frederico Salas, Leslie Salmon, Jim Sandifer, Linda Sasser, Lisa Schreiber, Mary Segovia, Abe Shames, Debra Shaw, Stephanie Shipp, Pat Singh, Mary Sklavos, Donna Stark, Claire Cocoran Stehling, Lynn Sweeden, Joy Tesh, Sue Thompson, Christine Tierney, Laura Topete, Carmen Villanueva, Laura Webber, Renée Weiss, Beth Winningham, Cindy Wislofsky, Judy Wood, Paula Yerman.

A special thanks to Marna Shulberg and the students of the Saticoy Branch of Van Nuys Community Adult School.

We would also like to thank the following individuals and organizations who provided their expertise:

Carl Abato, Alan Goldman, Dr. Larry Falk, Caroll Gray, Henry Haskell, Susan Haskell, Los Angeles Fire Department, Malcolm Loeb, Barbara Lozano, Lorne Dubin, United Farm Workers.

Authors' Acknowledgments

Throughout our careers as English language teachers, we have found inspiration in many places—in the classroom with our remarkable students, at schools, conferences, and workshops with our fellow teachers, and with our colleagues at the ESL Teacher Institute. We are grateful to be part of this international community.

We would like to sincerely thank and acknowledge Eliza Jensen, the project's Senior Editor. Without Eliza, this book would not have been possible. Her indomitable spirit, commitment to clarity, and unwavering advocacy allowed us to realize the book we envisioned.

Creating this dictionary was a collaborative effort and it has been our privilege to work with an exceptionally talented group of individuals who, along with Eliza Jensen, make up the Oxford Picture Dictionary team. We deeply appreciate the contributions of the following people:

Lynn Luchetti, Art Director, whose aesthetic sense and sensibility guided the art direction of this book,

Susan Brorein, Senior Designer, who carefully considered the design of each and every page,

Klaus Jekeli, Production Editor, who pored over both manuscript and art to ensure consistency and accuracy, and

Tracy Hammond, Art Buyer, who skillfully managed thousands of pieces of art and reference material.

We also want to thank Susan Mazer, the talented artist who was by our side for the initial problem-solving and Mary Chandler who also lent her expertise to the project.

We have learned much working with Marjorie Fuchs, Lori Howard, and Renée Weiss, authors of the dictionary's ancillary materials. We thank them for their on-going contributions to the dictionary program.

We must make special mention of Susan Lanzano, Editorial Manager, whose invaluable advice, insights, and queries were an integral part of the writing process.

This book is dedicated to my husband, Neil Reichline, who has encouraged me to take the road less traveled, and to my sons, Eli and Alex, who have allowed me to sit at their baseball games with my yellow notepad. —NS

This book is lovingly dedicated to my husband, Gary and my daughter, Emily Rose, both of whom hugged me tight and let me work into the night. —JAG

A Letter to the Teacher

Welcome to The Oxford Picture Dictionary.

This comprehensive vocabulary resource provides you and your students with over 3,700 words, each defined by engaging art and presented in a meaningful context. *The Oxford Picture Dictionary* enables your students to learn and use English in all aspects of their daily lives. The 140 key topics cover home and family, the workplace, the community, health care, and academic studies. The topics are organized into 12 thematic units that are based on the curriculum of beginning and low-intermediate level English language coursework. The word lists of the dictionary include both single word entries and verb phrases. Many of the prepositions and adjectives are presented in phrases as well, demonstrating the natural use of words in conjunction with one another.

The Oxford Picture Dictionary uses a variety of visual formats, each suited to the topic being represented. Where appropriate, word lists are categorized and pages are divided into sections, allowing you to focus your students' attention on one aspect of a topic at a time.

Within the word lists:

* nouns, adjectives, prepositions, and adverbs are numbered,

* verbs are bolded and identified by letters, and

* targeted prepositions and adjectives within phrases are bolded.

The dictionary includes a variety of exercises and self-access tools that will guide your students toward accurate and fluent use of the new words.

* Exercises at the bottom of the pages provide vocabulary development through pattern practice, application of the new language to other topics, and personalization questions.

* An alphabetical index assists students in locating all words and topics in the dictionary.

* A phonetic listing for each word in the index and a pronunciation guide give students the key to accurate pronunciation.

* A verb index of all the verbs presented in the dictionary provides students with information on the present, past, and past participle forms of the verbs.

The Oxford Picture Dictionary is the core of *The Oxford Picture Dictionary Program* which includes a *Dictionary Cassette,* a *Teacher's Book* and its companion *Focused Listening Cassette, Beginning* and *Intermediate Workbooks, Classic Classroom Activities* (a photocopiable activity book), *Overhead Transparencies,* and *Read All About It 1* and *2.* Bilingual editions of *The Oxford Picture Dictionary* are available in Spanish, Chinese, Vietnamese, and many other languages.

TEACHING THE VOCABULARY

Your students' needs and your own teaching philosophy will dictate how you use *The Oxford Picture Dictionary* with your students. The following general guidelines, however, may help you adapt the dictionary's pages to your particular course and students. (For topic-specific, step-by-step guidelines and activities for presenting and practicing the vocabulary on each dictionary page see the *Oxford Picture Dictionary Teacher's Book.*)

Preview the topic

A good way to begin any lesson is to talk with students to determine what they already know about the topic. Some different ways to do this are:

* Ask general questions related to the topic;

* Have students brainstorm a list of words they know from the topic; or

* Ask questions about the picture(s) on the page.

Present the vocabulary

Once you've discovered which words your students already know, you are ready to focus on presenting the words they need. Introducing 10–15 new words in a lesson allows students to really learn the new words. On pages where the word lists are longer, and students are unfamiliar with many of the words, you may wish to introduce the words by categories or sections, or simply choose the words you want in the lesson.

Here are four different presentation techniques. The techniques you choose will depend on the topic being studied and the level of your students.

* Say each new word and describe or define it within the context of the picture.

* Demonstrate verbs or verb sequences for the students, and have volunteers demonstrate the actions as you say them.

* Use Total Physical Response commands to build comprehension of the vocabulary: *Put the pencil on your book. Put it on your notebook. Put it on your desk.*

* Ask a series of questions to build comprehension and give students an opportunity to say the new words:

- ▶ Begin with *yes/no* questions. *Is #16 chalk?* (yes)

- ▶ Progress to *or* questions. *Is #16 chalk or a marker?* (chalk)

- ▶ Finally ask *Wh* questions.

  What can I use to write on this paper? (a marker/ Use a marker.)

Check comprehension

Before moving on to the practice stage, it is helpful to be sure all students understand the target vocabulary. There are many different things you can do to check students' understanding. Here are two activities to try:

- Tell students to open their books and point to the items they hear you say. Call out target vocabulary at random as you walk around the room checking to see if students are pointing to the correct pictures.

- Make true/false statements about the target vocabulary. Have students hold up two fingers for true, three fingers for false. *You can write with a marker.* [two fingers] *You raise your notebook to talk to the teacher.* [three fingers]

Take a moment to review any words with which students are having difficulty before beginning the practice activities.

Practice the vocabulary

Guided practice activities give your students an opportunity to use the new vocabulary in meaningful communication. The exercises at the bottom of the pages are one source of guided practice activities.

- **Talk about...** This activity gives students an opportunity to practice the target vocabulary through sentence substitutions with meaningful topics.

  e.g. **Talk about your feelings.**

    I feel <u>happy</u> when I see my friends.

- **Practice...** This activity gives students practice using the vocabulary within common conversational functions such as making introductions, ordering food, making requests, etc.

  e.g. **Practice asking for things in the dining room.**

    Please pass <u>the platter</u>.

    May I have <u>the creamer</u>?

    Could I have <u>a fork</u>, please?

- **Use the new language.** This activity asks students to brainstorm words within various categories, or may

ask them to apply what they have learned to another topic in the dictionary. For example, on *Colors*, page 12, students are asked to look at *Clothing I*, pages 64–65, and name the colors of the clothing they see.

- **Share your answers.** These questions provide students with an opportunity to expand their use of the target vocabulary in personalized discussion. Students can ask and answer these questions in whole class discussions, pair or group work, or they can write the answers as journal entries.

Further guided and communicative practice can be found in the *Oxford Picture Dictionary Teacher's Book* and in *Classic Classroom Activities*. The *Oxford Picture Dictionary Beginning* and *Intermediate Workbooks* and *Read All About It 1* and *2* provide your students with controlled and communicative reading and writing practice.

We encourage you to adapt the materials to suit the needs of your classes, and we welcome your comments and ideas. Write to us at:

Oxford University Press
ESL Department
198 Madison Avenue
New York, NY 10016

Jayme Adelson-Goldstein

Norma Shapiro

A Letter to the Student

Dear Student of English,

Welcome to *The Oxford Picture Dictionary*. The more than 3,700 words in this book will help you as you study English.

Each page in this dictionary teaches about a specific topic. The topics are grouped together in units. All pages in a unit have the same color and symbol. For example, each page in the Food unit has this symbol:

On each page you will see pictures and words. The pictures have numbers or letters that match the numbers or letters in the word lists. Verbs (action words) are identified by letters and all other words are identified by numbers.

How to find words in this book

- Use the Table of Contents, pages ix–xi.
  Look up the general topic you want to learn about.

- Use the Index, pages 173–205.
  Look up individual words in alphabetical (A–Z) order.

- Go topic by topic.
  Look through the book until you find something that interests you.

How to use the Index

When you look for a word in the index this is what you will see:

the word   the number (or letter) in the word list

apples [ăp/əlz] **50**–4

the pronunciation   the page number

If the word is on one of the maps, pages 122–125, you will find it in the Geographical Index on pages 206–208.

How to use the Verb Guide

When you want to know the past form of a verb or its past participle form, look up the verb in the verb guide. The regular verbs and their spelling changes are listed on pages 170–171. The simple form, past form, and past participle form of irregular verbs are listed on page 172.

Workbooks

There are two workbooks to help you practice the new words:
The Oxford Picture Dictionary Beginning and *Intermediate Workbooks.*

As authors and teachers we both know how difficult English can be (and we're native speakers!). When we wrote this book, we asked teachers and students from the U.S. and other countries for their help and ideas. We hope their ideas and ours will help you. Please write to us with your comments or questions at:

Oxford University Press
ESL Department
198 Madison Avenue
New York, NY 10016

We wish you success!

Jayme Adelson-Goldstein   Norma Shapiro

給學生的一封信

各位學習英文的學生大家好，

歡迎使用 *The Oxford Picture Dictionary*（牛津圖解辭典）。 本辭典所收錄的 詞目超過 3,700個， 對您學習英文有莫大的助益。

本辭典中的每一頁都有一個特定的主題。 幾個不同的主題會結合成一個單元。 所有同一單元內的頁數都使用相同的顏色和符號。 舉例來說， 食物單元內的每一頁都使用這個符號：

每一頁的內容是以圖示和詞目來編排。 所有的圖示都以數字或英文字母編號， 並與詞目的數字或英文字母編號相同。 除動詞 （動作用字） 是以英文字母標示外， 其它詞目皆以數字來編號。

如何查檢詞目

- 使用目錄 （第 ix–xi 頁）
  查檢您想知道的主題。

- 使用索引 （第 173–205 頁）
  按英文字母順序 (A–Z) 查檢個別單。

- 按主題翻查
  翻查辭典直到找到您感興趣的內容。

如何使用索引

從索引中查檢單詞， 您會看到：

單詞　　　　單詞表中的數字 (或字母)

apples [ăp/əlz] **50–4**

頁號

如果這個單詞在第 122–125 頁中的其中一張地圖上， 您可以在第 206–208 頁內的地理索引中找到該單詞。

如何使用動詞指引

如果您想知道某一個動詞的過去式或者過去分詞， 不妨查檢動詞指引。 規則動詞及其拼法變化列在第 170–171 頁。 不規則動詞的簡單式、 過去式和過去分詞則列在第 172 頁。

練習本

本辭典也隨附兩本練習本， 協助您學習新字：
The Oxford Picture Dictionary Beginning 和 *Intermediate Workbooks*（牛津圖解辭典初級和中級練習本）.

身為作者及教師， 我們都知道學習英文的困難 （英文還是我們的母語呢！）。 我們在編排這本辭典時， 曾向美國及其它國家的教師和學生尋求協助及徵詢意見。 我們希望大家的集思廣益能協助讀者學好英文。 如有任何建議或問題， 歡迎您來信賜教：

Oxford University Press
ESL Department
198 Madison Avenue
New York, NY 10016

祝您學習有成！

Jayme Adelson-Goldstein　　　Norma Shapiro

Contents 目錄

Contents　目錄

10. Plants and Animals 植物及動物

11. Work 工作

12. Recreation 娛樂

1. chalkboard
黑板

2. screen
螢幕

3. student
學生

4. overhead projector
投影機

5. teacher
教師

6. desk
書桌

7. chair/seat
椅子／座位

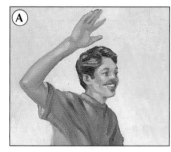

A. Raise your hand.
舉手。

B. Talk to the teacher.
與老師談話。

C. Listen to a cassette.
聽錄音帶。

D. Stand up.
站起來。

E. Sit down./Take a seat.
坐下。

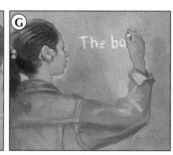

F. Point to the picture.
指向圖畫。

G. Write on the board.
寫在黑板上。

H. Erase the board.
擦黑板。

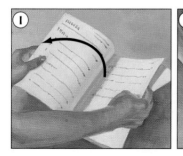

I. Open your book.
打開書本。

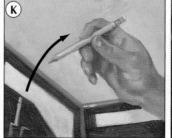

J. Close your book.
圖上書本。

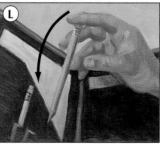

K. Take out your pencil.
拿出鉛筆。

L. Put away your pencil.
收好鉛筆。

8. bookcase
書架

9. globe
地球儀

10. clock
時鐘

11. cassette player
錄放音機

12. map
地圖

13. pencil sharpener
削鉛筆刀

14. bulletin board ['buləθn]
佈告欄

15. computer
電腦

16. chalk
粉筆

17. chalkboard eraser
黑板擦

18. pen
筆

19. marker
色筆

20. pencil
鉛筆

21. pencil eraser
鉛筆橡皮擦

22. textbook
教科書

23. workbook
練習本

24. binder/notebook
活頁筆記本

25. notebook paper
筆記本活頁紙

26. spiral notebook
螺線型筆記本

27. ruler
量尺

28. dictionary
辭典

29. picture dictionary
圖解辭典

30. the alphabet
字母

31. numbers
數字

Use the new language.

1. Name three things you can open.

2. Name three things you can put away.

3. Name three things you can write with.

Share your answers.

1. Do you like to raise your hand?

2. Do you ever listen to cassettes in class?

3. Do you ever write on the board?

3

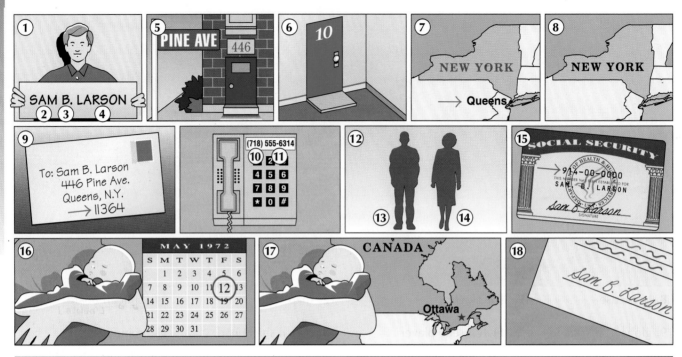

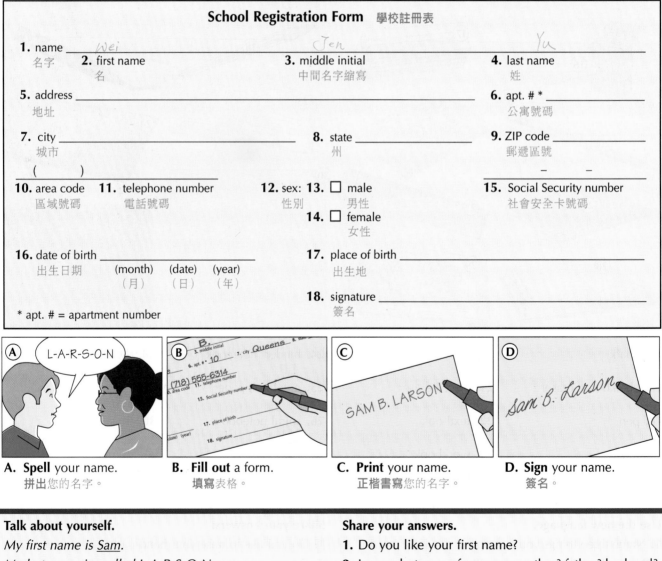

School Registration Form 學校註冊表

1. name *Wei*   *Jen*   *Yu*
   名字
   2. first name   **3.** middle initial   **4.** last name
   名   中間名字縮寫   姓

5. address _____ **6.** apt. # * _____
   地址   公寓號碼

7. city _____ **8.** state _____ **9.** ZIP code _____
   城市   州   郵遞區號

   (   ) _____   ___ – ___ – ___

10. area code   **11.** telephone number   **12.** sex: **13.** ☐ male   **15.** Social Security number
    區域號碼   電話號碼   性別   男性   社會安全卡號碼
                                          14. ☐ female
                                             女性

16. date of birth _____ **17.** place of birth _____
    出生日期   (month)   (date)   (year)   出生地
              （月）   （日）   （年）

                              18. signature _____
                                           簽名

* apt. # = apartment number

A. Spell your name.   **B. Fill out** a form.   **C. Print** your name.   **D. Sign** your name.
拼出您的名字。   填寫表格。   正楷書寫您的名字。   簽名。

Talk about yourself.

My first name is Sam.

My last name is spelled L-A-R-S-O-N.

I come from Ottawa.

Share your answers.

1. Do you like your first name?

2. Is your last name from your mother? father? husband?

3. What is your middle name?

1. classroom 教室	**7.** lockers 更衣室	**13.** principal's office 校長室
2. teacher 教師	**8.** rest rooms 廁所	**14.** principal 校長
3. auditorium [ˌɔdəˈtorɪəm] 禮堂	**9.** gym 健身室	**15.** counselor's office 輔導室
4. cafeteria _snack bar_ 自助餐廳 _restaurant_	**10.** bleachers 露天看臺 (球場)	**16.** counselor [ˈkaʊnslɚ] 輔導員
5. lunch benches 午餐長凳	**11.** track 跑道	**17.** main office 大辦公室
6. library 圖書館	**12.** field 操場	**18.** clerk 職員

More vocabulary

instructor: teacher

coach: gym teacher

administrator: principal or other school supervisor

Share your answers.

1. Do you ever talk to the principal of your school?

2. Is there a place for you to eat at your school?

3. Does your school look the same or different from the one in the picture?

5

Dictionary work 查字典

A. Look up a word.
查生字。

B. Read the word.
讀生字。

C. Say the word.
唸出生字。

D. Repeat the word.
再唸一次生字。

E. Spell the word.
拼生字。

F. Copy the word.
抄寫生字。

Work with a partner 與他人一起學習

G. Ask a question.
提出問題。

H. Answer a question.
回答問題。

I. Share a book.
共用書本。

J. Help your partner.
協助您的夥伴。

Work in a group 團體學習

K. Brainstorm a list.
盡腦力想出項目。

L. Discuss the list.
列出事項。

M. Draw a picture.
畫圖。

N. Dictate a sentence.
句子聽寫。

Class work 教室活動

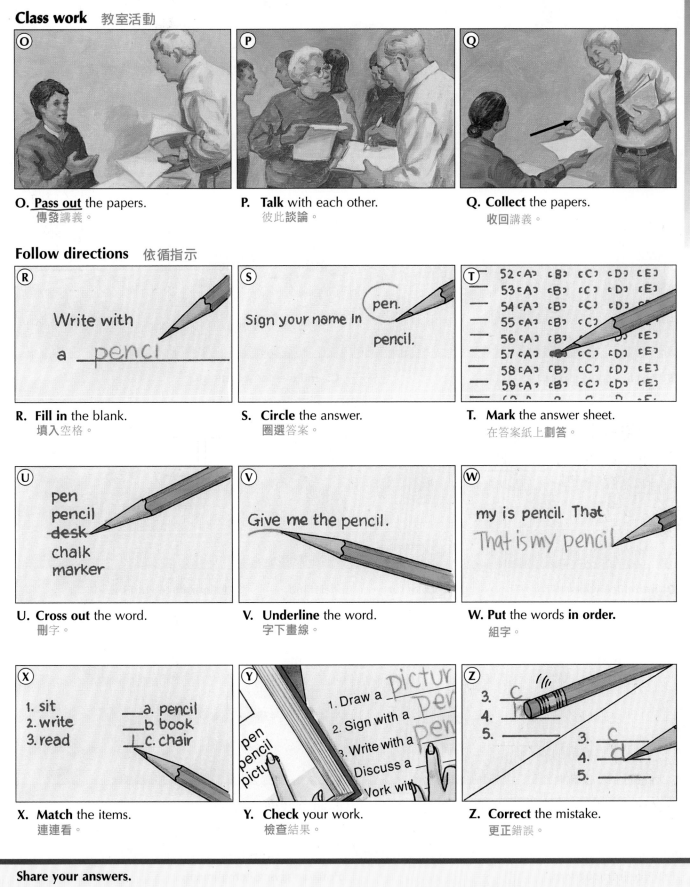

O. <u>Pass out</u> the papers.
傳發講義。

P. **Talk** with each other.
彼此談論。

Q. **Collect** the papers.
收回講義。

Follow directions 依循指示

R. **Fill in** the blank.
填入空格。

S. **Circle** the answer.
圈選答案。

T. **Mark** the answer sheet.
在答案紙上劃答。

U. **Cross out** the word.
刪字。

V. **Underline** the word.
字下畫線。

W. **Put** the words **in order.**
組字。

X. **Match** the items.
連連看。

Y. **Check** your work.
檢查結果。

Z. **Correct** the mistake.
更正錯誤。

Share your answers.

1. Do you like to work in groups?

2. Do you like to share books?

3. Do you like to answer questions?

4. Is it easy for you to talk with your classmates?

5. Do you always check your work?

6. Do you cross out your mistakes or erase them?

A. greet someone
打招呼

B. begin a conversation
開始交談

C. end the conversation
結束交談

D. introduce yourself
自我介紹

E. make sure you **understand**
確認您所聽到的

F. introduce your friend
介紹您的朋友

G. compliment your friend
稱讚您的朋友

H. thank your friend
向朋友致謝

I. apologize
道歉

Practice introductions.

Hi, I'm Sam Jones and this is my friend, Pat Green.

Nice to meet you. I'm Tomas Garcia.

Practice giving compliments.

That's a great sweater, Tomas.

Thanks Pat. I like your shoes.

Look at **Clothing I**, pages **64–65** for more ideas.

1. telephone / phone
   電話
2. receiver
   聽筒
3. cord
   電話線
4. local call
   本地電話
5. long-distance call
   長途電話
6. international call
   國際電話
7. operator
   接線生
8. directory assistance (411)
   查號台 (411)
9. emergency service (911)
   緊急服務 (911)
10. phone card
    電話卡
11. pay phone
    公用電話
12. cordless phone
    無線電話
13. cellular phone
    行動電話
14. answering machine
    電話答錄機
15. telephone book
    電話簿
16. pager
    傳呼機

Using a pay phone 使用公用電話

A. **Pick up** the receiver.
   拿起聽筒。
B. **Listen** for the dial tone.
   聆聽是否有通話鈴響。
C. **Deposit** coins.
   投入硬幣。
D. **Dial** the number.
   撥號碼。
E. **Leave** a message.
   留話。
F. **Hang up** the receiver.
   掛上聽筒。

More vocabulary

When you get a person or place that you didn't want to call, we say you have the **wrong number.**

Share your answers.

1. What kinds of calls do you make?
2. How much does it cost to call your country?
3. Do you like to talk on the telephone?

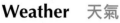

Weather 天氣

Temperature
溫度

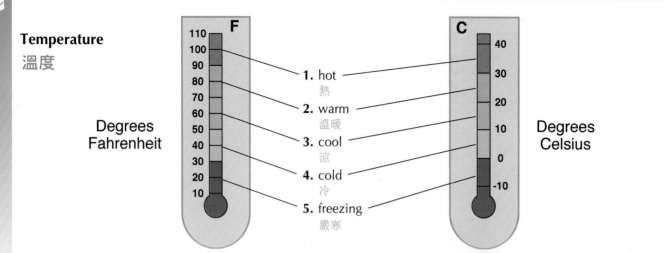

Degrees
Fahrenheit

Degrees
Celsius

1. hot
熱

2. warm
溫暖

3. cool
涼

4. cold
冷

5. freezing
嚴寒

6. sunny / clear
晴天

7. cloudy
陰天

8. raining
下雨

9. snowing
下雪

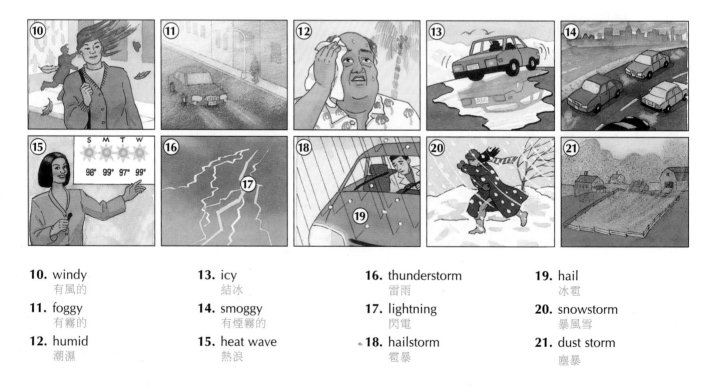

10. windy
有風的

11. foggy
有霧的

12. humid
潮濕

13. icy
結冰

14. smoggy
有煙霧的

15. heat wave
熱浪

16. thunderstorm
雷雨

17. lightning
閃電

18. hailstorm
雹暴

19. hail
冰雹

20. snowstorm
暴風雪

21. dust storm
塵暴

Language note: *it is, there is*

For **1–14** we use,   *It's <u>cloudy</u>.*

For **15–21** we use,   *There's <u>a heat wave</u>.*
                     There's <u>lightning</u>.

Talk about the weather.

Today it's <u>hot</u>. It's <u>98 degrees</u>.

Yesterday it was <u>warm</u>. It was <u>85 degrees</u>.

1. **little** hand
小手

2. **big** hand
大手

3. **fast** driver
開快車的司機

4. **slow** driver
開慢車的司機

5. **hard** chair
硬墊椅子

6. **soft** chair
軟墊椅子

7. **thick** book/
fat book
厚書

8. **thin** book
薄書

9. **full** glass
盛滿的杯子

10. **empty** glass
空杯子

11. **noisy** children/
loud children
吵鬧的孩童

12. **quiet** children
安靜的孩童

13. **heavy** box
重盒子

14. **light** box
輕盒子

15. **neat** closet
整齊的櫃子

16. **messy** closet
髒亂的櫃子

17. **good** dog
好狗

18. **bad** dog
壞狗

19. **expensive** ring
昂貴的戒指

20. **cheap** ring
便宜的戒指

21. **beautiful** view
美麗的景緻

22. **ugly** view
難看的景緻

23. **easy** problem
簡單的問題

24. **difficult** problem/
hard problem
困難的問題

Use the new language.

1. Name three things that are thick.
2. Name three things that are soft.
3. Name three things that are heavy.

Share your answers.

1. Are you a slow driver or a fast driver?
2. Do you have a neat closet or a messy closet?
3. Do you like loud or quiet parties?

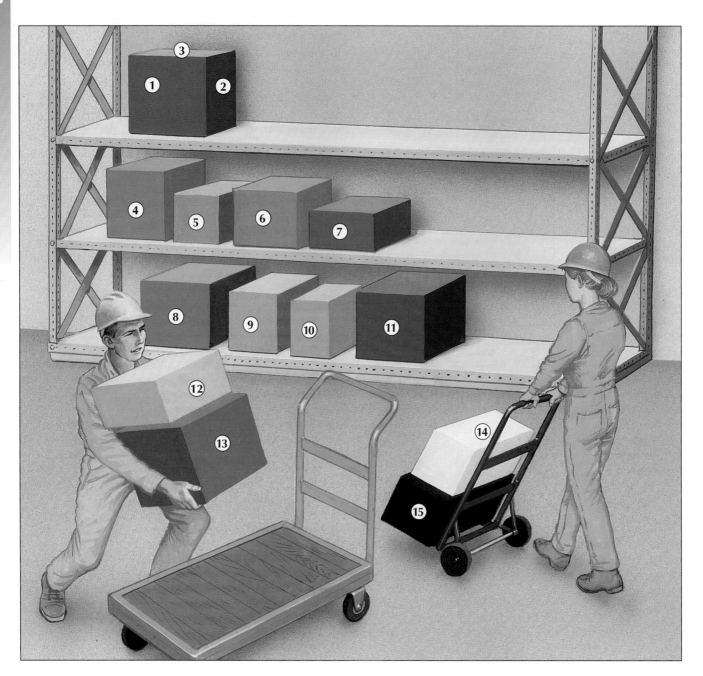

1. blue 藍色	**6.** orange 橘色	**11.** brown 棕色
2. dark blue 深藍色	**7.** purple 紫色	**12.** yellow 黃色
3. light blue 淡藍色	**8.** green 綠色	**13.** red 紅色
4. turquoise 藍綠色	**9.** beige 米色	**14.** white 白色
5. gray 灰色	**10.** pink 粉紅色	**15.** black 黑色

Use the new language.

Look at **Clothing I**, pages **64–65**.

Name the colors of the clothing you see.

That's <u>a dark blue suit</u>.

Share your answers.

1. What colors are you wearing today?

2. What colors do you like?

3. Is there a color you don't like? What is it?

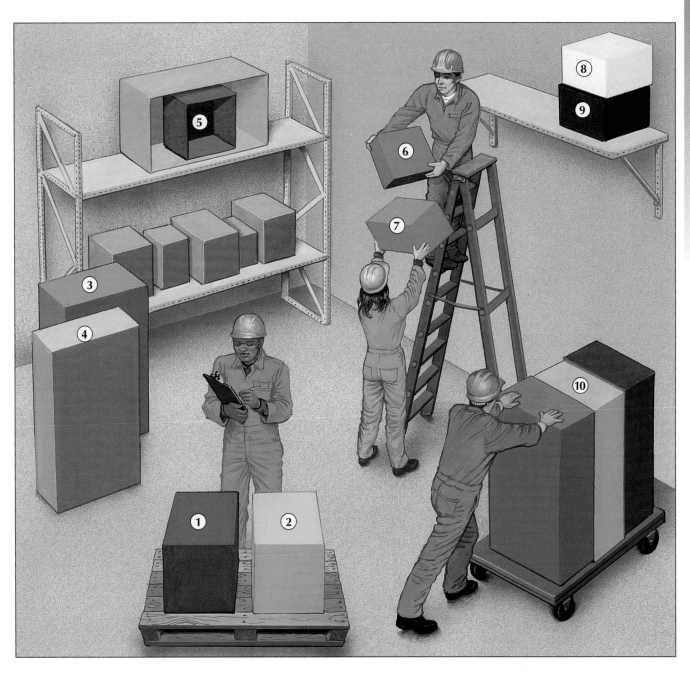

1. The red box is **next to** the yellow box, **on the left.**
   紅色盒子在黃色盒子的**旁邊**，**也就是左側**。

2. The yellow box is **next to** the red box, **on the right.**
   黃色盒子在紅色盒子的**旁邊**，**也就是右側**。

3. The turquoise box is **behind** the gray box.
   藍綠色盒子在灰色盒子的**後面**。

4. The gray box is **in front of** the turquoise box.
   灰色盒子在藍綠色盒子的**前面**。

5. The dark blue box is **in** the beige box.
   深藍色盒子在米色盒子的**裡面**。

6. The green box is **above** the orange box.
   綠色盒子在橘色盒子的**上方**。

7. The orange box is **below** the green box.
   橘色盒子在綠色盒子的**下方**。

8. The white box is **on** the black box.
   白色盒子在黑色盒子的**上方**。

9. The black box is **under** the white box.
   黑色盒子在白色盒子的**下方**。

10. The pink box is **between** the purple box and the brown box.
    粉紅色盒子在紫色盒子和棕色盒子**之間**。

More vocabulary

near: in the same area
*The white box is **near** the black box.*

far from: not near
*The red box is **far from** the black box.*

Cardinals 基數

0 zero 零	11 eleven 十一	21 twenty-one 二十一	101 one hundred one 一百零一
1 one 一	12 twelve 十二	22 twenty-two 二十二	1,000 one thousand 一千
2 two 二	13 thirteen 十三	30 thirty 三十	1,001 one thousand one 一千零一
3 three 三	14 fourteen 十四	40 forty 四十	10,000 ten thousand 一萬
4 four 四	15 fifteen 十五	50 fifty 五十	100,000 one hundred thousand 十萬
5 five 五	16 sixteen 十六	60 sixty 六十	1,000,000 one million 一百萬
6 six 六	17 seventeen 十七	70 seventy 七十	1,000,000,000 one billion 十億
7 seven 七	18 eighteen 十八	80 eighty 八十	
8 eight 八	19 nineteen 十九	90 ninety 九十	
9 nine 九	20 twenty 二十	100 one hundred 一百	
10 ten 十			

Ordinals 序數 (日期)

1st first 第一	8th eighth 第八	15th fifteenth 第十五
2nd second 第二	9th ninth 第九	16th sixteenth 第十六
3rd third 第三	10th tenth 第十	17th seventeenth 第十七
4th fourth 第四	11th eleventh 第十一	18th eighteenth 第十八
5th fifth 第五	12th twelfth 第十二	19th nineteenth 第十九
6th sixth 第六	13th thirteenth 第十三	20th twentieth 第二十
7th seventh 第七	14th fourteenth 第十四	

Roman numerals 羅馬數字

I = 1	VII = 7	XXX = 30
II = 2	VIII = 8	XL = 40
III = 3	IX = 9	L = 50
IV = 4	X = 10	C = 100
V = 5	XV = 15	D = 500
VI = 6	XX = 20	M = 1,000

Fractions 分數

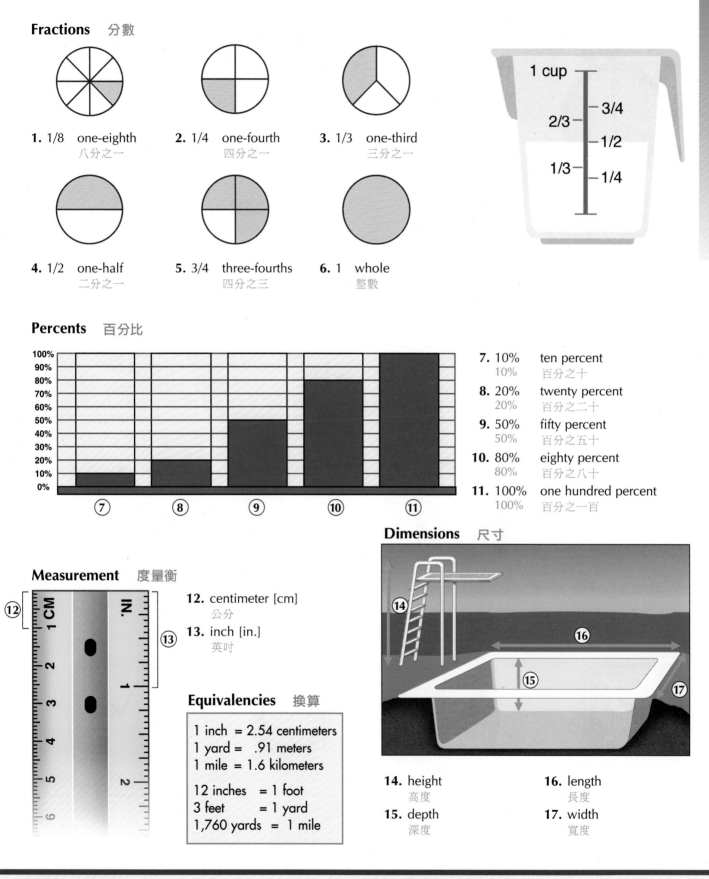

1. 1/8 one-eighth
八分之一

2. 1/4 one-fourth
四分之一

3. 1/3 one-third
三分之一

4. 1/2 one-half
二分之一

5. 3/4 three-fourths
四分之三

6. 1 whole
整數

1 cup
3/4
2/3
1/2
1/3
1/4

Percents 百分比

7. 10% ten percent
10% 百分之十

8. 20% twenty percent
20% 百分之二十

9. 50% fifty percent
50% 百分之五十

10. 80% eighty percent
80% 百分之八十

11. 100% one hundred percent
100% 百分之一百

Measurement 度量衡

12. centimeter [cm]
公分

13. inch [in.]
英吋

Equivalencies 換算

1 inch = 2.54 centimeters
1 yard = .91 meters
1 mile = 1.6 kilometers

12 inches = 1 foot
3 feet   = 1 yard
1,760 yards = 1 mile

Dimensions 尺寸

14. height
高度

15. depth
深度

16. length
長度

17. width
寬度

More vocabulary

measure: to find the size or amount of something

count: to find the total number of something

Share your answers.

1. How many students are in class today?

2. Who was the first person in class today?

3. How far is it from your home to your school?

1. second
秒

2. minute
分

3. hour
小時

A.M.

P.M.

4. 1:00
one o'clock
一點鐘

5. 1:05
one-oh-five
一點五分
five after one
一點過五分

6. 1:10
one-ten
一點十分
ten after one
一點過十分

7. 1:15
one-fifteen
一點十五分
a quarter after one
一點過一刻

8. 1:20
one-twenty
一點二十
twenty after one
一點過二十分

9. 1:25
one twenty-five
一點二十五分
twenty-five after one
一點過二十五分

10. 1:30
one-thirty
一點三十分
half past one
一點半

11. 1:35
one thirty-five
一點三十五分
twenty-five to two
差二十五分兩點

12. 1:40
one-forty
一點四十分
twenty to two
差二十分兩點

13. 1:45
one forty-five
一點四十五分
a quarter to two
差一刻兩點

14. 1:50
one-fifty
一點五十分
ten to two
差十分兩點

15. 1:55
one fifty-five
一點五十五分
five to two
差五分兩點

Talk about the time.

What time is it? It's <u>10:00 a.m.</u>

What time do you wake up on weekdays? At <u>6:30 a.m.</u>

What time do you wake up on weekends? At <u>9:30 a.m.</u>

Share your answers.

1. How many hours a day do you study English?

2. You are meeting friends at 1:00. How long will you wait for them if they are late?

16. morning
上午

17. noon
中午

18. afternoon
下午

19. evening
傍晚

20. night
晚上

21. midnight
午夜

22. early
早

23. late
遲

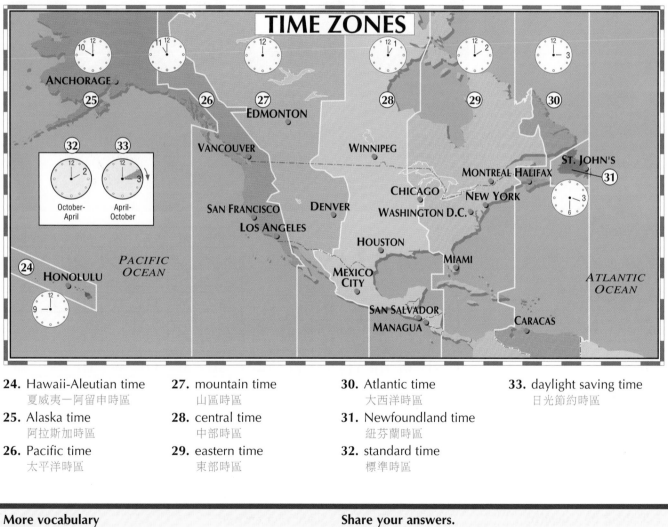

TIME ZONES

24. Hawaii-Aleutian time
夏威夷—阿留申時區

25. Alaska time
阿拉斯加時區

26. Pacific time
太平洋時區

27. mountain time
山區時區

28. central time
中部時區

29. eastern time
東部時區

30. Atlantic time
大西洋時區

31. Newfoundland time
紐芬蘭時區

32. standard time
標準時區

33. daylight saving time
日光節約時區

More vocabulary

on time: not early and not late
*He's **on time.***

Share your answers.

1. When do you watch television? study?
   do housework?

2. Do you come to class on time? early? late?

Days of the week
星期幾

1. Sunday
星期日

2. Monday
星期一

3. Tuesday
星期二

4. Wednesday
星期三

5. Thursday
星期四

6. Friday
星期五

7. Saturday
星期六

8. year
年

9. month
月

10. day
日

11. week
星期

12. weekdays
週一至週五

13. weekend
週末

14. date
日期

15. today
今天

16. tomorrow
明天

17. yesterday
昨天

18. last week
上個星期

19. this week
這個星期

20. next week
下個星期

21. every day
每天

22. once a week
一星期一次

23. twice a week
一星期兩次

24. three times a week
一星期三次

2001 ⑧ ⑨ ◆ JANUARY ◆ **2001**

① SUN	② MON	③ TUE	④ WED	⑤ THU	⑥ FRI	⑦ SAT
	⑩ 1	2	3	4	5	6
7	8	9	10	11	12	13
14	15	16	⑪ 17	18	19	20
21	22	23	⑫ 24	25	26	⑬ 27
28	29	30	31			

THE DAILY TIMES
MAY 10, 2001

◆ MAY ◆

SU	M	TU	W	TH	F	SA
⑱ 1	2	3	4	5	6	7
⑲ 8	9	10	11	12	13	14
⑳ 15	16	17	18	19	20	21
22	23	24	25	26	27	28

Talk about the calendar.

What's today's date? It's <u>March 10th</u>.

What day is it? It's <u>Tuesday</u>.

What day was yesterday? It was <u>Monday</u>.

Share your answers.

1. How often do you come to school?

2. How long have you been in this school?

2001

JAN ㉕
SUN	MON	TUE	WED	THU	FRI	SAT
	1	2	3	4	5	6
7	8	9	10	11	12	13
14	15	16	17	18	19	20
21	22	23	24	25	26	27
28	29	30	31			

FEB ㉖
SUN	MON	TUE	WED	THU	FRI	SAT
				1	2	3
4	5	6	7	8	9	10
11	12	13	14	15	16	17
18	19	20	21	22	23	24
25	26	27	28			

MAR ㉗
SUN	MON	TUE	WED	THU	FRI	SAT
				1	2	3
4	5	6	7	8	9	10
11	12	13	14	15	16	17
18	19	20	21	22	23	24
25	26	27	28	29	30	31

APR ㉘
SUN	MON	TUE	WED	THU	FRI	SAT
1	2	3	4	5	6	7
8	9	10	11	12	13	14
15	16	17	18	19	20	21
22	23	24	25	26	27	28
29	30					

MAY ㉙
SUN	MON	TUE	WED	THU	FRI	SAT
		1	2	3	4	5
6	7	8	9	10	11	12
13	14	15	16	17	18	19
20	21	22	23	24	25	26
27	28	29	30	31		

JUN ㉚
SUN	MON	TUE	WED	THU	FRI	SAT
					1	2
3	4	5	6	7	8	9
10	11	12	13	14	15	16
17	18	19	20	21	22	23
24	25	26	27	28	29	30

JUL ㉛
SUN	MON	TUE	WED	THU	FRI	SAT
1	2	3	4	5	6	7
8	9	10	11	12	13	14
15	16	17	18	19	20	21
22	23	24	25	26	27	28
29	30	31				

AUG ㉜
SUN	MON	TUE	WED	THU	FRI	SAT
			1	2	3	4
5	6	7	8	9	10	11
12	13	14	15	16	17	18
19	20	21	22	23	24	25
26	27	28	29	30	31	

SEP ㉝
SUN	MON	TUE	WED	THU	FRI	SAT
						1
2	3	4	5	6	7	8
9	10	11	12	13	14	15
16	17	18	19	20	21	22
23/30	24	25	26	27	28	29

OCT ㉞
SUN	MON	TUE	WED	THU	FRI	SAT
	1	2	3	4	5	6
7	8	9	10	11	12	13
14	15	16	17	18	19	20
21	22	23	24	25	26	27
28	29	30	31			

NOV ㉟
SUN	MON	TUE	WED	THU	FRI	SAT
				1	2	3
4	5	6	7	8	9	10
11	12	13	14	15	16	17
18	19	20	21	22	23	24
25	26	27	28	29	30	

DEC ㊱
SUN	MON	TUE	WED	THU	FRI	SAT
						1
2	3	4	5	6	7	8
9	10	11	12	13	14	15
16	17	18	19	20	21	22
23/30	24/31	25	26	27	28	29

MARCH 21 ㊲

JUNE 21 ㊳

SEPT. 21 ㊴

DEC. 21 ㊵

JUNE 5 TIM! ㊶

MARCH 2 ANNIVERSARY ㊷

JULY 4 INDEPENDENCE DAY STATE BANK CLOSED-JULY 4 ㊸

APRIL 4 EASTER SUNDAY ㊹

MAY 17 DOCTOR 4:30 ㊺

AUGUST ㊻

Months of the year
月份

25. January
一月

26. February
二月

27. March
三月

28. April
四月

29. May
五月

30. June
六月

31. July
七月

32. August
八月

33. September
九月

34. October
十月

35. November
十一月

36. December
十二月

Seasons
季節

37. spring
春天

38. summer
夏天

39. fall
秋天

40. winter
冬天

41. birthday
生日

42. anniversary
週年紀念

43. legal holiday
法定假日

44. religious holiday
宗教假日

45. appointment
約會

46. vacation
度假

Use the new language.

Look at the **ordinal numbers** on page **14**.

Use ordinal numbers to say the date.

It's June 5th. It's the fifth.

Talk about your birthday.

My birthday is in the winter.

My birthday is in January.

My birthday is on January twenty-sixth.

Coins 硬幣

1. $.01 = 1¢
a penny/1 cent
一分

2. $.05 = 5¢
a nickel/5 cents
五分

3. $.10 = 10¢
a dime/10 cents
十分

4. $.25 = 25¢
a quarter/25 cents
兩毛五分

5. $.50 = 50¢
a half dollar
五毛

6. $1.00
a silver dollar
一元硬幣

Bills 紙幣

7. $1.00
a dollar
一元

8. $5.00
five dollars
五元

9. $10.00
ten dollars
十元

10. $20.00
twenty dollars
二十元

11. $50.00
fifty dollars
五十元

12. $100.00
one hundred dollars
一百元

Ways to pay 付錢方式

13. cash
現金

14. personal check
個人支票

15. credit card
信用卡

16. money order
匯票

17. traveler's check
旅行支票

More vocabulary

borrow: to get money from someone and return it later

lend: to give money to someone and get it back later

pay back: to return the money that you borrowed

Other ways to talk about money:

a dollar bill or *a one*

a five-dollar bill or *a five*

a ten-dollar bill or *a ten*

a twenty-dollar bill or *a twenty*

A. shop for
購物

B. sell
銷售

C. pay for/**buy**
付錢／購買

D. give
給

E. keep
持有

F. return
退回

G. exchange
交換

1. price tag
標價

2. regular price
一般價格

3. sale price
折扣售價

4. bar code
條碼

5. receipt
收據

6. price/cost
價格

7. sales tax
營業稅

8. total
總計

9. change
找錢

More vocabulary

When you use a credit card to shop, you get a **bill** in the mail. Bills list, in writing, the items you bought and the total you have to pay.

Share your answers.

1. Name three things you pay for every month.

2. Name one thing you will buy this week.

3. Where do you like to shop?

1. children
孩童

2. baby
嬰兒

3. toddler
幼兒

4. 6-year-old boy
六歲男孩

5. 10-year-old girl
十歲女孩

6. teenagers
青少年

7. 13-year-old boy
十三歲男孩

8. 19-year-old girl
十九歲女孩

9. adults
成年人

10. woman
女人

11. man
男人

12. senior citizen
老年人

13. young
年輕

14. middle-aged
中年

15. elderly
老年

16. tall
高

17. average height
一般高度

18. short
矮

19. pregnant
懷孕

20. heavyset
重體型

21. average weight
一般體重

22. thin/slim
瘦／苗條

23. attractive
好看

24. cute
可愛

25. physically challenged
肢體殘障

26. sight impaired/blind
視力障礙／視盲

27. hearing impaired/deaf
聽力障礙／耳聾

Talk about yourself and your teacher.

I am young, average height, and average weight.

My teacher is a middle-aged, tall, thin man.

Use the new language.

Turn to **Hobbies and Games**, pages **162–163**.

Describe each person on the page.

He's a heavyset, short, senior citizen.

1. short hair 短頭髮	**8.** bangs 瀏海	**15.** black hair 黑髮
2. shoulder-length hair 及肩頭髮	**9.** straight hair 直髮	**16.** blond hair 金髮
3. long hair 長頭髮	**10.** wavy hair 波浪髮	**17.** brown hair 棕髮
4. part 分髮	**11.** curly hair 捲髮	**18.** brush 刷子
5. mustache 小鬍子	**12.** bald 禿頭	**19.** scissors 剪刀
6. beard 大鬍子	**13.** gray hair 白頭髮	**20.** blow dryer 吹風機
7. sideburns 側鬚	**14.** red hair 紅髮	**21.** rollers 髮捲

22. comb
梳子

A. **cut** hair
剪髮

B. **perm** hair
燙髮

C. **set** hair
上髮捲

D. **color** hair/**dye** hair
染髮

More vocabulary

hair stylist: a person who cuts, sets, and perms hair

hair salon: the place where a hair stylist works

Talk about your hair.

My hair is long, straight, and brown.

I have long, straight, brown hair.

When I was a child my hair was short, curly, and blond.

Tom Lee's Family

1. grandparents
祖父母

Min   Lu

2. grandmother   **3.** grandfather
祖母   祖父

4. parents
父母

Rose   Chang   Helen   Daniel

Tom

5. mother   **6.** father   **10.** aunt   **11.** uncle
母親   父親   姑媽   姑父

Lily   Alex   Emily

8. sister   **9.** brother   **12.** cousin
姊／妹   兄／弟   表姊／妹

7. (Min and Lu's)
grandson
Min和 Lu的
孫子

Berta   Mario   Ana Garcia's
Family

Ana

13. mother-in-law   **14.** father-in-law
婆婆   公公

Marta   Carlos   Tito   **20.** (Tito's) wife
Tito的 太太

15. sister-in-law   **16.** brother-in-law   **19.** husband
兄嫂／弟婦   大伯／小叔   先生

Alice   Eddie   Sara   Felix

17. niece   **18.** nephew   **21.** daughter   **22.** son
姪女   姪子   女兒   兒子

More vocabulary

Lily and Emily are Min and Lu's **granddaughters**.
Daniel is Min and Lu's **son-in-law**.
Ana is Berta and Mario's **daughter-in-law**.

Share your answers.

1. How many brothers and sisters do you have?
2. What number son or daughter are you?
3. Do you have any children?

Lisa Smith's Family

23. married
已婚

Carol *Dan*

Lisa

24. divorced
離婚

25. single mother
單親母親

26. single father
單親父親

27. remarried
再婚

Rick *Carol*

Dan *Sue*

Rick *Carol*

28. stepfather
繼父

David *Mary*

29. half brother
同母異父弟弟

30. half sister
同母異父妹妹

Lisa

Dan *Sue*

31. stepmother
繼母

Kim *Bill*

32. stepsister
繼母以前婚姻中
所生的姐妹

33. stepbrother
繼母以前婚姻中
所生的兄弟

More vocabulary

Carol is Dan's **former wife**.

Sue is Dan's **wife**.

Dan is Carol's **former husband**.

Rick is Carol's **husband**.

Lisa is the **stepdaughter** of both Rick and Sue.

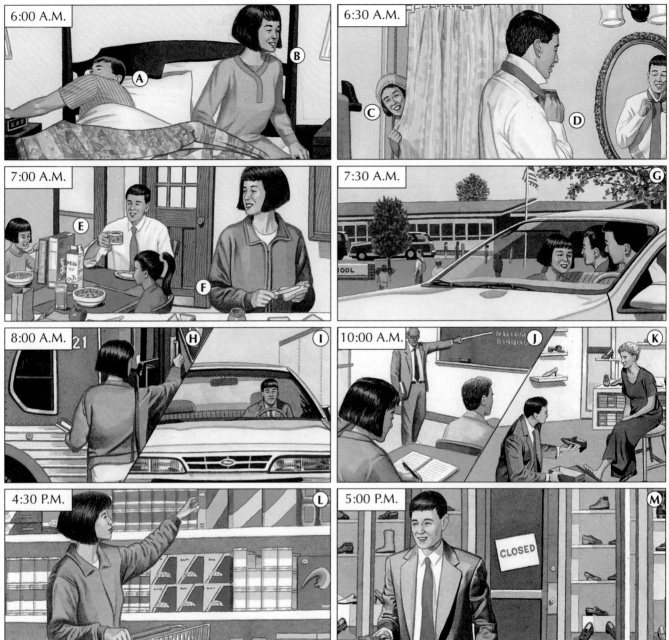

A. **wake up**
睡醒

B. **get up**
起床

C. **take** a shower
淋浴

D. **get dressed**
穿衣服

E. **eat** breakfast
吃早餐

F. **make** lunch
準備午餐

G. **take** the children to school
送孩子到學校

H. **take** the bus to school
搭車到學校

I. **drive** to work/**go** to work
開車上班／去上班

J. **be** in school
在學校

K. **work**
工作

L. **go** to the market
去市場

M. **leave** work
下班

Grammar point: 3rd person singular

For **he** and **she**, we add **-s** or **-es** to the verb.

*He/She wake**s** up.*

*He/She watch**es** TV.*

These verbs are different (irregular):

be   *He/She **is** in school at 10:00 a.m.*

have   *He/She **has** dinner at 6:30 p.m.*

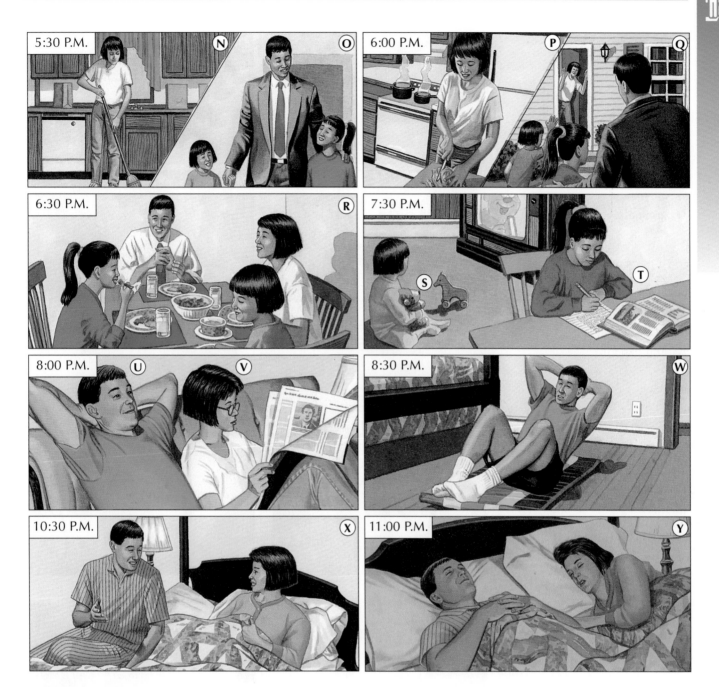

N. clean the house
清理房子

O. pick up the children
接孩子

P. cook dinner
作晚飯

Q. come home／**get** home
回家

R. have dinner
吃晚飯

S. watch TV
看電視

T. do homework
作家庭作業

U. relax
放輕鬆

V. read the paper
看報

W. exercise
運動

X. go to bed
上床

Y. go to sleep
睡覺

Talk about your daily routine.

I take a shower in the morning.

I go to school in the evening.

I go to bed at 11 o'clock.

Share your answers.

1. Who makes dinner in your family?

2. Who goes to the market?

3. Who goes to work?

Life Events 生活記事

A. **be born**
出生

B. **start** school
入學

C. **immigrate**
移民

D. **graduate**
畢業

E. **learn** to drive
學開車

F. **join** the army
服兵役

G. **get** a job
就業

H. **become** a citizen
入籍公民

I. **rent** an apartment
租公寓

J. **go** to college
上大學

K. **fall in love**
談戀愛

L. **get married**
結婚

Grammar point: past tense

start		immigrate		be	— was	have	— had
learn		graduate		get	— got	buy	— bought
join	+ed	move	+d	become	— became		
rent		retire		go	— went		
travel		die		fall	— fell		

These verbs are different (irregular):

28

M. have a baby
生兒育女

N. travel
旅行

O. buy a house
購屋

P. move
搬家

Q. have a grandchild
獲得孫兒（女）

R. die
死亡

1. birth certificate
   出生證明
2. diploma
   文憑
3. Resident Alien card
   居留卡
4. driver's license
   駕駛執照
5. Social Security card
   社會安全卡
6. Certificate of Naturalization
   入籍歸化證明
7. college degree
   大學文憑
8. marriage license
   結婚許可證
9. passport
   護照

More vocabulary

When a husband dies, his wife becomes a **widow**.
When a wife dies, her husband becomes a **widower**.
When older people stop working, we say they **retire**.

Talk about yourself.

I was born in 1968.
I learned to drive in 1987.
I immigrated in 1990.

1. hot
   熱
2. thirsty
   渴
3. sleepy
   想睡覺

4. cold
   冷
5. hungry
   餓
6. full
   飽

7. comfortable
   舒服
8. uncomfortable
   不舒服
9. disgusted
   作嘔
10. calm
    冷靜
11. nervous
    緊張

12. in pain
    痛苦
13. worried
    擔憂
14. sick
    生病
15. well
    感覺舒服
16. relieved
    舒解

17. hurt
    傷心
18. lonely
    寂寞
19. in love
    戀愛

More vocabulary
furious: very angry
terrified: very scared
overjoyed: very happy

[I'm burned out.
    exhausted: very tired
    starving: very hungry
    humiliated: very embarrassed

Talk about your feelings.
I feel <u>happy</u> when I see <u>my friends</u>.
I feel <u>homesick</u> when I think about <u>my family</u>.

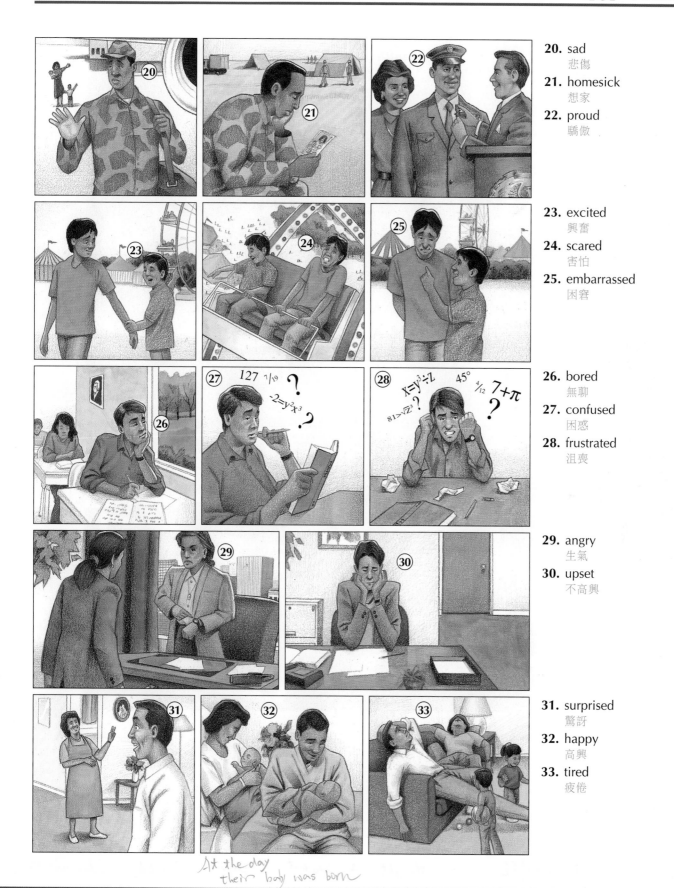

20. sad
    悲傷
21. homesick
    想家
22. proud
    驕傲

23. excited
    興奮
24. scared
    害怕
25. embarrassed
    困窘

26. bored
    無聊
27. confused
    困惑
28. frustrated
    沮喪

29. angry
    生氣
30. upset
    不高興

31. surprised
    驚訝
32. happy
    高興
33. tired
    疲倦

At the day their baby was born

Use the new language.

Look at **Clothing I**, page **64** and answer the questions.

1. How does the runner feel?
2. How does the man at the bus stop feel?
3. How does the woman at the bus stop feel?
4. How do the teenagers feel?
5. How does the little boy feel?

The Ceremony

1. graduating class
   畢業班
2. gown
   禮服
3. cap
   畢業帽
4. stage
   舞台

5. <u>podium</u>
   講台
6. graduate
   畢業生
7. diploma
   文憑
8. <u>valedictorian</u>
   畢業致詞人

9. guest speaker
   來賓致詞人
10. audience
    觀眾
11. photographer
    攝影師
A. **graduate**
   畢業

B. **applaud / clap**
   拍手／鼓掌
C. **cry**
   哭
D. **take** a picture
   照相
E. **give** a speech
   致詞

Honor Roll student 榮譽榜學生   Straight A Student   Dean's list 優異榜   who's who 博公知名人

Talk about what the people in the pictures are doing.

She is
- tak**ing** a picture.
- giv**ing** a speech.
- smil**ing**.
- laugh**ing**.

He is
- mak**ing** a toast.
- clap**ping**.

They are
- graduat**ing**.
- hug**ging**.
- kiss**ing**.
- applaud**ing**.

The Party

12. caterer
包辦餐飲者

13. buffet
自助餐

14. guests
賓客

15. banner
旗幟

16. dance floor
舞池

17. DJ (disc jockey)
DJ音樂主持人

18. gifts
禮物

F. kiss
吻

G. hug
擁抱

H. laugh
歡笑

I. make a toast
舉杯頌祝

J. dance
跳舞

year book 畢業紀念冊
prom 畢業舞會
college ring 大學戒指

Share your answers.

1. Did you ever go to a graduation? Whose?

2. Did you ever give a speech? Where?

3. Did you ever hear a great speaker? Where?

4. Did you ever go to a graduation party?

5. What do you like to eat at parties?

6. Do you like to dance at parties?

33

Places to Live 居所

1. the city / an urban area
城市／市區

2. the suburbs
郊區

3. a small town
小鎮

4. the country / a rural area
鄉村／鄉野地區

5. apartment building
公寓大樓

6. house
獨棟房子

7. townhouse
雙併房子

8. mobile home
汽車房屋

9. college dormitory
大學宿舍

10. shelter
收容所 避難所

11. nursing home
養老院

12. ranch
牧場

13. farm
農場

More vocabulary

duplex house: a house divided into two homes

condominium: an apartment building where each apartment is owned separately

co-op: an apartment building owned by the residents

Share your answers.

1. Do you like where you live?

2. Where did you live in your country?

3. What types of housing are there near your school?

34

Renting an apartment 租公寓

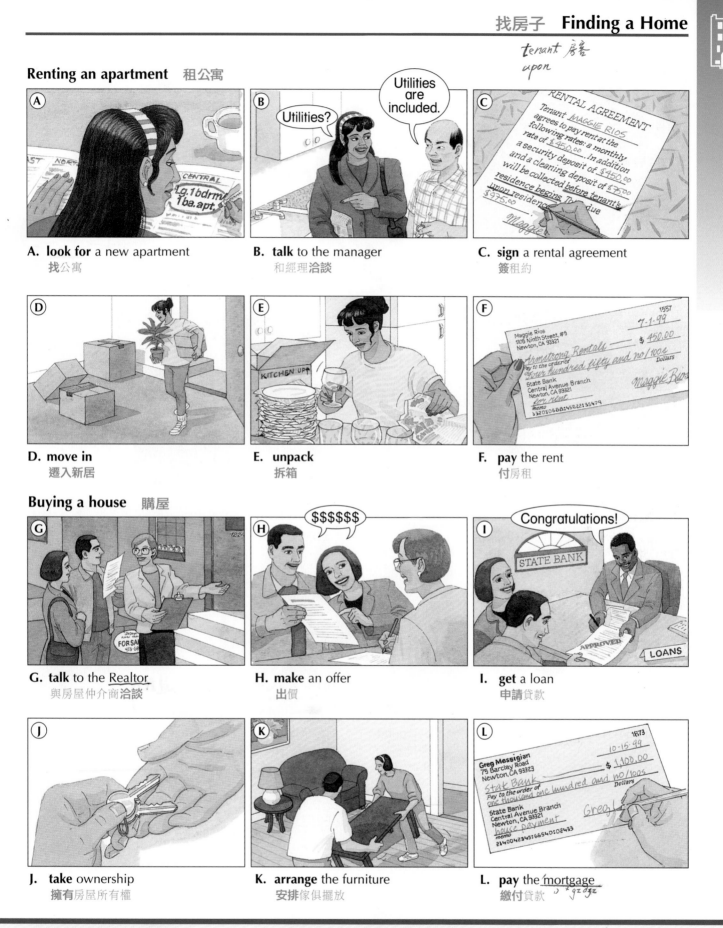

A. look for a new apartment
找公寓

B. talk to the manager
和經理洽談

C. sign a rental agreement
簽租約

D. move in
遷入新居

E. unpack
拆箱

F. pay the rent
付房租

Buying a house 購屋

G. talk to the Realtor
與房屋仲介商洽談

H. make an offer
出價

I. get a loan
申請貸款

J. take ownership
擁有房屋所有權

K. arrange the furniture
安排傢俱擺放

L. pay the mortgage
繳付貸款

More vocabulary

lease: a rental agreement for a specific period of time 租約

utilities: gas, water, and electricity for the home

Practice talking to an apartment manager.

How much is the rent?

Are utilities included?

When can I move in?

35

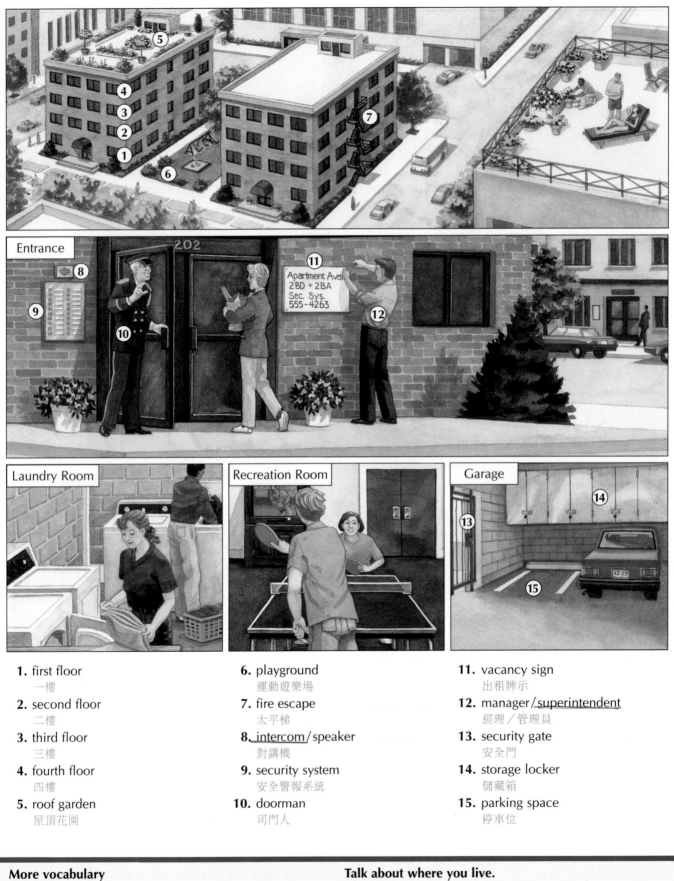

1. first floor
一樓

2. second floor
二樓

3. third floor
三樓

4. fourth floor
四樓

5. roof garden
屋頂花園

6. playground
運動遊樂場

7. fire escape
太平梯

8. intercom/speaker
對講機

9. security system
安全警報系統

10. doorman
司門人

11. vacancy sign
出租牌示

12. manager/superintendent
經理/管理員

13. security gate
安全門

14. storage locker
儲藏箱

15. parking space
停車位

More vocabulary

rec room: a short way of saying **recreation room**

basement: the area below the street level of an apartment or a house

Talk about where you live.

I live in Apartment 3 near the entrance.

I live in Apartment 11 on the second floor near the fire escape.

16. swimming pool
游泳池

17. balcony
陽台

18. courtyard
庭院／天井

19. air conditioner
冷氣機

20. trash bin
垃圾箱

21. alley
巷

22. neighbor
鄰居

23. fire exit
緊急出口

24. trash chute
垃圾滑運槽

25. smoke detector
煙霧警報器

26. stairway
樓梯

27. peephole   *peep show*
窺孔

28. door chain
門鍊

29. dead-bolt lock
內拴鎖

30. doorknob
門把

31. key
鑰匙

32. landlord   *landlady 房東*
房東

33. tenant   *red light district*
房客

34. elevator
電梯

35. stairs
樓梯

36. mailboxes
信箱

Grammar point: *there is, there are*
singular: *there is*   plural: *there are*
There is a fire exit in the hallway.
There are mailboxes in the lobby.

Talk about apartments.
My apartment has <u>an elevator</u>, <u>a lobby</u>, and <u>a rec room</u>.
My apartment doesn't have <u>a pool</u> or <u>a garage</u>.
My apartment needs <u>air conditioning</u>.

1. floor plan
建築平面圖

2. backyard
後院

3. fence
圍籬

4. mailbox
信箱

5. driveway
車道

6. garage
車房

7. garage door
車房門

8. screen door
紗門

9. porch light
走廊燈

10. doorbell
門鈴

11. front door
前門

12. storm door
防暴風雨用的重型門

13. steps
階梯

14. front walk
前門走道

15. front yard
前院

16. deck
庭院甲板

17. window
窗戶

18. shutter
窗扇

19. gutter
屋頂邊溝

20. roof
屋頂

21. chimney
煙囪

22. TV antenna
電視天線

More vocabulary

two-story house: a house with two floors

downstairs: the bottom floor

upstairs: the part of a house above the bottom floor

Share your answers.

1. What do you like about this house?

2. What's something you don't like about the house?

3. Describe the perfect house.

1. hedge
   樹籬

2. hammock
   吊床

3. garbage can
   垃圾桶

4. leaf blower
   吹葉器

5. patio furniture
   庭院傢俱

6. patio
   庭院台

7. barbecue grill
   烤肉架

8. sprinkler
   灑水器

9. hose
   水管

10. compost pile
    堆肥

11. rake
    耙子

12. hedge clippers
    修籬剪

13. shovel
    鏟子

14. trowel
    小鏟子

15. pruning shears
    修枝剪

16. wheelbarrow
    獨輪手推車

17. watering can
    澆水壺

18. flowerpot
    花盆

19. flower
    花朵

20. bush
    灌木

21. lawn
    草坪

22. lawn mower
    割草機

A. **weed** the flower bed
   除雜草

B. **water** the plants
   澆花

C. **mow** the lawn
   割草

D. **plant** a tree
   植樹

E. **trim** the hedge
   修樹籬

F. **rake** the leaves
   耙樹葉

Talk about your yard and gardening.

I like to plant trees.

I don't like to weed.

I like/don't like to work in the yard/garden.

Share your answers.

1. What flowers, trees, or plants do you see in the picture? (Look at **Trees, Plants, and Flowers**, pages **128–129** for help.)

2. Do you ever use a barbecue grill to cook?

1. cabinet 廚櫃	**8.** shelf 廚架	**15.** toaster oven 烤麵包機兼烤箱	**22.** counter 流理臺
2. paper towels 大紙巾	**9.** refrigerator 冰箱	**16.** pot 鍋子	**23.** drawer 抽屜
3. dish drainer 盤碟滴乾板	**10.** freezer 冰庫	**17.** teakettle 燒茶壺	**24.** pan 平底鍋
4. dishwasher 洗碗機	**11.** coffeemaker 煮咖啡器	**18.** stove 火爐	**25.** electric mixer 電動攪拌器
5. garbage disposal 廢物處理機	**12.** blender 攪碎機	**19.** burner 爐頭	**26.** food processor 食物處理器
6. sink 水槽	**13.** microwave oven 微波爐烤箱	**20.** oven 烤箱	**27.** cutting board 切菜板
7. toaster 烤麵包機	**14.** electric can opener 電動開罐器	**21.** broiler 烤培爐	

Talk about the location of kitchen items.

The toaster oven is *on the counter* *near the stove*.

The microwave is *above the stove*.

Share your answers.

1. Do you have a garbage disposal? a dishwasher? a microwave?

2. Do you eat in the kitchen?

1. **china cabinet**
   餐具五斗櫃

2. **set of dishes**
   整套餐碟

3. **platter**
   餐盤

4. **ceiling fan**
   天花板扇

5. **light fixture**
   電燈裝置

6. **serving dish**
   餐盤

7. **candle**
   蠟燭

8. **candlestick**
   燭臺

9. **vase**
   花瓶

10. **tray**
    托盤

11. **teapot**
    茶壺

12. **sugar bowl**
    糖罐

13. **creamer**
    奶脂罐

14. **saltshaker**
    鹽瓶

15. **pepper shaker**
    胡椒瓶

16. **dining room chair**
    用餐坐椅

17. **dining room table**
    餐桌

18. **tablecloth**
    桌布

19. **napkin**
    餐巾

20. **place mat**
    餐具墊

21. **fork**
    叉子

22. **knife**
    刀

23. **spoon**
    湯匙

24. **plate**
    盤子

25. **bowl**
    碗

26. **glass**
    玻璃杯

27. **coffee cup**
    咖啡杯

28. **mug**
    馬克杯

Practice asking for things in the dining room.

Please pass <u>the platter</u>.

May I have <u>the creamer</u>?

Could I have <u>a fork</u>, please?

Share your answers.

1. What are the women in the picture saying?

2. In your home, where do you eat?

3. Do you like to make dinner for your friends?

A Living Room 起居室

1. bookcase
   書架

2. basket
   籃子

3. track lighting
   調動燈光

4. lightbulb
   燈泡

5. ceiling
   天花板

6. wall
   牆壁

7. painting
   圖畫

8. mantel
   壁爐臺

9. fireplace
   壁爐

10. fire
    爐火

11. fire screen
    爐火簾

12. logs
    木頭

13. wall unit
    壁櫥

14. stereo system
    音響系統

15. floor lamp
    立燈

16. drapes
    布簾

17. window
    窗戶

18. plant
    植物

19. sofa/couch
    沙發

20. throw pillow
    抱枕

21. end table
    小茶几

22. magazine holder
    雜誌置放籃

23. coffee table
    大茶几

24. armchair/easy chair
    搖椅

25. love seat   *love chair*
    雙人沙發座   情趣椅

26. TV (television)
    電視機

27. carpet
    地毯

food fight
Slumber party. 小女孩的睡衣聚会
pillow fight

Use the new language.

Look at **Colors**, page **12**, and describe this room.

There is a gray sofa and a gray armchair.

Talk about your living room.

In my living room I have a sofa, two chairs, and a coffee table.

I don't have a fireplace or a wall unit.

1. <u>hamper</u>
換洗衣服籃

2. bathtub
浴缸

3. <u>rubber mat</u>
橡膠墊

4. drain
排水

5. hot water
熱水

6. faucet
水龍頭

7. cold water
冷水

8. <u>towel rack</u>
毛巾架

9. tile
瓷磚

10. showerhead
蓮蓬頭

11. (mini)blinds
（小型）百葉窗

12. bath towel
浴巾

13. hand towel
擦手巾

14. washcloth
擦洗巾

15. toilet paper
衛生紙

16. toilet brush
馬桶刷

17. toilet
馬桶

18. mirror
鏡子

19. medicine cabinet
藥櫃

20. toothbrush
牙刷

21. toothbrush holder
牙刷座台

22. sink
洗臉槽

23. soap
香皂

24. soap dish
香皂盒

25. wastebasket
垃圾桶

26. scale
體重器

27. bath mat
浴墊

plunger 通馬桶塞

More vocabulary

half bath: a bathroom without a shower or bathtub

置物櫃 **linen closet:** a closet or cabinet for towels and sheets

stall shower: a shower without a bathtub 衛生紙

沖水浴室

Share your answers.

1. Do you turn off the water when you brush your teeth? wash your hair? shave?

2. Does your bathroom have a bathtub or a stall shower?

1. mirror
   鏡子

2. dresser / bureau
   衣櫃／五斗櫃

3. drawer
   抽屜

4. closet
   衣櫥

5. curtains
   窗簾

6. window shade
   窗扇

7. photograph
   相片

8. bed
   床

9. pillow
   枕頭

10. pillowcase
    枕頭套

11. bedspread
    床罩

12. blanket
    被毯

13. flat sheet
    床單

14. fitted sheet
    床單罩

15. headboard
    床頭板

16. clock radio
    時鐘收音機

17. lamp
    檯燈

18. lampshade
    燈罩

19. light switch
    電燈開關

20. outlet
    插座

21. night table
    床頭桌

22. dust ruffle
    床墊裙罩

23. rug
    小地毯

24. floor
    地板

25. mattress
    床墊

26. box spring
    彈簧床墊

27. bed frame
    床架

Use the new language.

Describe this room. (See **Describing Things**, page **11**, for help.)

I see a soft pillow and a beautiful bedspread.

Share your answers.

1. What is your favorite thing in your bedroom?

2. Do you have a clock in your bedroom? Where is it?

3. Do you have a mirror in your bedroom? Where is it?

1. bunk bed
雙層床

2. comforter
棉被

3. night-light
夜燈

4. mobile
旋吊玩飾

5. wallpaper
壁紙

6. crib
嬰兒床

7. bumper pad
嬰兒床圍墊

8. chest of drawers
抽屜式衣櫃

9. baby monitor
嬰兒監視器

10. teddy bear
泰迪熊

11. smoke detector
煙霧警報器

12. changing table
尿布更換台

13. diaper pail
尿布桶

14. dollhouse
娃娃屋

15. blocks
積木

16. ball
球

17. picture book
相簿

18. doll
娃娃

19. cradle
搖籃

20. coloring book
著色簿

21. crayons
粉蠟筆

22. puzzle
拼圖

23. stuffed animals
填塞玩具

24. toy chest
玩具箱

meal plan 餐券.   room mate 題.   suite mate 寢室題.

Talk about where items are in the room.

The dollhouse is near *the coloring book.*
The teddy bear is on *the chest of drawers.*

Share your answers.

1. Do you think this is a good room for children? Why?
2. What toys did you play with when you were a child?
3. What children's stories do you know?

45

A. **dust** the furniture
拭去像俱上的灰塵

B. **recycle** the newspapers
回收報紙

C. **clean** the oven
清理烤箱

D. **wash** the windows
擦洗窗戶

E. **sweep** the floor
打掃地板

F. **empty** the wastebasket
清理字紙簍

G. **make** the bed
舖床

H. **put away** the toys
放好玩具

I. **vacuum** the carpet
吸地毯

J. **mop** the floor
拖地板

K. **polish** the furniture
擦光傢俱

L. **scrub** the floor
擦洗地板

M. **wash** the dishes
洗碗盤

N. **dry** the dishes
拭乾碗盤

O. **wipe** the counter
擦拭料理臺

P. **change** the sheets
換床單

Q. **take out** the garbage
倒垃圾

Talk about yourself.

I wash the dishes every day.

I change the sheets every week.

I never dry the dishes.

Share your answers.

1. Who does the housework in your family?

2. What is your favorite cleaning job?

3. What is your least favorite cleaning job?

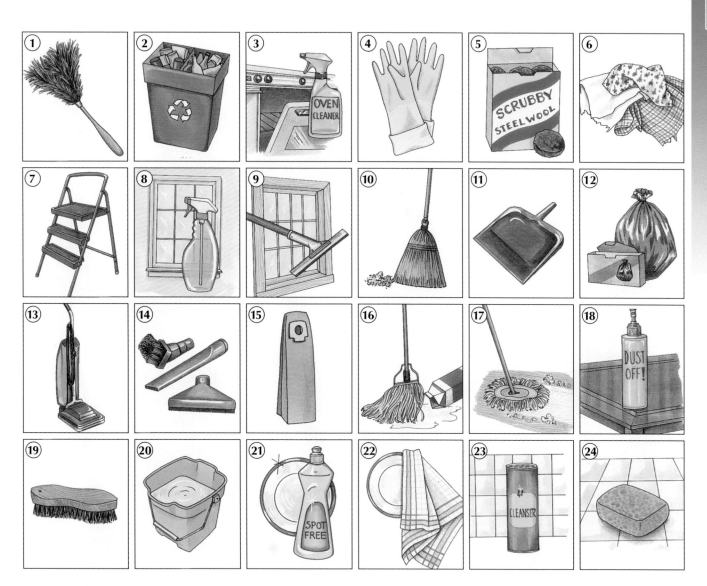

1. feather duster
   羽毛撢子

2. recycling bin
   資源回收桶

3. oven cleaner
   烤箱清潔劑

4. rubber gloves
   橡皮手套

5. steel-wool soap pads
   鋼絲棉肥皂墊

6. rags
   抹布

7. stepladder
   梯凳

8. glass cleaner
   玻璃清潔劑

9. squeegee
   橡皮刷

10. broom
    掃帚

11. dustpan
    畚箕

12. trash bags
    垃圾袋

13. vacuum cleaner
    吸塵器

14. vacuum cleaner attachments
    吸塵器附件

15. vacuum cleaner bag
    吸塵袋

16. wet mop
    溼拖把

17. dust mop
    除塵拖把

18. furniture polish
    傢俱亮光劑

19. scrub brush
    擦洗刷

20. bucket/pail
    水桶

21. dishwashing liquid
    洗碗精

22. dish towel
    擦碗巾

23. cleanser
    清潔劑

24. sponge
    海綿

Practice asking for the items.

I want to <u>wash the windows</u>.

Please hand me <u>the squeegee</u>.

I have to <u>sweep the floor</u>.

Can you get me <u>the broom</u>, please?

1. The water heater is **not working**.
   火爐**壞了**。

2. The power is **out**.
   停電了。

3. The roof is **leaking**.
   屋頂**漏水**。

4. The wall is **cracked**.
   牆壁**有裂縫**。

5. The window is **broken**.
   窗戶**破了**。

6. The lock is **broken**.
   鎖**壞了**。

7. The steps are **broken**.
   階梯**壞了**。

8. roofer
   修屋頂工人

9. electrician
   電器技師

10. repair person
    修理匠

11. locksmith
    鎖匠

12. carpenter
    木匠

13. fuse box
    保險絲盒

14. gas meter
    煤氣計錶

Use the new language.

Look at **Tools and Building Supplies**, pages **150–151**.

Name the tools you use for household repairs.

I use a hammer and nails to fix a broken step.

I use a wrench to repair a dripping faucet.

15. The furnace is **broken**.
火爐**壞了**。

16. The faucet is **dripping**.
水龍頭**漏水**。

17. The sink is **overflowing**.
水槽**堵塞**。

18. The toilet is **stopped up**.
馬桶**阻塞**。

19. The pipes are **frozen**.
水管**凍結**。

20. plumber
裝修水管工

21. exterminator
滅蟲人員

Household pests
家居害蟲

22. termite(s)
白蟻

23. flea(s)
跳蚤

24. ant(s)
螞蟻

25. cockroach(es)
蟑螂

26. mice*
（小）老鼠

27. rat(s)
（大）老鼠

*Note: *one mouse, two mice*

More vocabulary

fix: to repair something that is broken

exterminate: to kill household pests

pesticide: a chemical that is used to kill household pests

Share your answers.

1. Who does household repairs in your home?
2. What is the worst problem a home can have?
3. What is the most expensive problem a home can have?

TODAY

BANANAS 2lb/1.00
BLUEBERRIES 1.99 pint

1. grapes
葡萄

2. pineapples
鳳梨

3. bananas
香蕉

4. apples
蘋果

5. peaches
桃子

6. pears
梨子

7. apricots
杏子

8. plums
李子

9. grapefruit
葡萄柚

10. oranges
柳橙

11. lemons
檸檬

12. limes
酸橙 莱姆

13. tangerines
柑橘 /tændʒə'rin/

14. avocadoes
酪梨

15. cantaloupes
甜瓜 /kæntə'lop/

16. cherries
櫻桃

17. strawberries
草莓

18. raspberries
蔗莓 覆盆子

19. blueberries
藍莓

20. papayas
木瓜

21. mangoes
芒果

22. coconuts
椰子

23. nuts
胡桃

24. watermelons
西瓜

25. dates
棗子

26. prunes /prun/
梅子乾

27. raisins
葡萄乾

28. not ripe
未成熟的

29. ripe
成熟的

30. rotten
腐爛的

Language note: *a bunch of*

We say *a bunch of grapes* and *a bunch of bananas*.

Share your answers.

1. Which fruits do you put in a fruit salad?

2. Which fruits are sold in your area in the summer?

3. What fruits did you have in your country?

TOMATOES .69/lb.

CORN 4/$1.00

1. lettuce
萵苣

2. cabbage
甘藍菜

3. carrots
胡蘿蔔

4. zucchini
夏南瓜

5. radishes
蘿蔔

6. beets /bit/
甜菜

7. sweet peppers
甜椒

8. chili peppers
辣椒

9. celery
芹菜

10. parsley
荷蘭芹

11. spinach
菠菜

12. cucumbers
黃瓜

13. squash /skwɑʃ/
西葫蘆 南瓜

14. turnips /tʃnəp/ 蘿蔔
大頭菜

15. broccoli
綠花椰菜

16. cauliflower
白花椰菜

17. scallions
蔥

18. eggplants
茄子

19. peas
豌豆

20. artichokes /ɑrtɪ.tʃok/
朝鮮薊

21. potatoes
馬鈴薯

22. yams
地瓜

23. tomatoes
番茄

24. asparagus
蘆筍

25. string beans
菜豆

26. mushrooms
香菇

27. corn
玉蜀黍

28. onions
洋蔥

29. garlic
大蒜

30. kimchi 泡菜

Language note: *a bunch of, a head of*

We say *a bunch of carrots, a bunch of celery,* and *a bunch of spinach.*

We say *a head of lettuce, a head of cabbage,* and *a head of cauliflower.*

Share your answers.

1. Which vegetables do you eat raw? cooked?

2. Which vegetables need to be in the refrigerator?

3. Which vegetables don't need to be in the refrigerator?

Beef 牛肉

1. roast beef
烘烤用牛肉

2. steak
牛排

3. stewing beef
燉煮用牛肉

4. ground beef
絞牛肉

5. beef ribs
牛排骨

6. veal cutlets
牛肉片

7. liver
牛肝

8. tripe
牛肚

Pork 豬肉

9. ham
火腿

10. pork chops
豬排

11. bacon
醃豬肉

12. sausage
香腸

Lamb 羊肉

13. lamb shanks
羊腿肉

14. leg of lamb
羊腿

15. lamb chops
羊排

16. chicken
雞肉

17. turkey
火雞肉

18. duck
鴨肉

19. breasts
雞胸肉

20. wings
雞翅膀

21. thighs
雞大腿

22. drumsticks
雞小腿

23. gizzards
內臟

24. raw chicken
生雞肉

25. cooked chicken
熟雞肉

More vocabulary

vegetarian: a person who doesn't eat meat

Meat and poultry without bones are called **boneless**.

Poultry without skin is called **skinless**.

Share your answers.

1. What kind of meat do you eat most often?

2. What kind of meat do you use in soup?

3. What part of the chicken do you like the most?

1. white bread
白麵包

2. wheat bread
小麥麵包

3. rye bread
裸麥麵包

4. smoked turkey
薰火雞肉

5. salami
義大利香腸

6. pastrami
腌薰牛肉

7. roast beef
烤牛肉

8. corned beef
腌牛肉

9. American cheese
美國乳酪

10. cheddar cheese
黃色硬乾酪

11. Swiss cheese
瑞士乳酪

12. jack cheese
傑克式乳酪

13. potato salad
馬鈴薯沙拉

14. coleslaw
碎菜沙拉

15. pasta salad
麵食沙拉

Fish 魚類

16. trout
鱒魚

17. catfish
鯰魚

18. whole salmon
整隻鮭魚

19. salmon steak
鮭魚排

20. halibut
比目魚

21. filet of sole
鰈魚(片)

Shellfish 貝類

22. crab
螃蟹

23. lobster
龍蝦

24. shrimp
蝦子

25. scallops
干貝

26. mussels
貽貝

27. oysters
牡蠣

28. clams
蛤

29. fresh fish
新鮮魚

30. frozen fish
冷凍魚

Practice ordering a sandwich.

I'd like <u>roast beef</u> and <u>American cheese</u> on <u>rye bread</u>.

Tell what you want on it.

Please put <u>tomato</u>, <u>lettuce</u>, <u>onions</u>, and <u>mustard</u> on it.

Share your answers.

1. Do you like to eat fish?

2. Do you buy fresh or frozen fish?

1. bottle return
退還瓶子

2. meat and poultry section
肉類和家禽部

3. shopping cart
購物車

4. canned goods
罐裝產品

5. aisle
走道

6. baked goods
烘烤食品

7. shopping basket
購物菜籃

8. manager
經理

9. dairy section
奶製品部門

10. pet food
寵物食品

11. produce section
蔬果部門

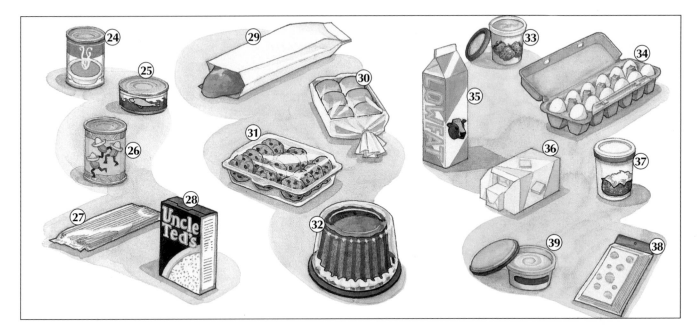

24. soup
湯罐頭

25. tuna
鮪魚罐頭

26. beans
青豆罐頭

27. spaghetti
義大利麵

28. rice
米

29. bread
麵包

30. rolls
小麵包

31. cookies
餅乾

32. cake
蛋糕

33. yogurt
酸奶酪

34. eggs
雞蛋

35. milk
牛奶

36. butter
牛油

37. sour cream
酸奶油

38. cheese
乳酪

39. margarine
植物奶油

12. frozen foods 冷凍食物	**15.** beverages 飲料	**18.** cash register 收銀機	**21.** bagger 裝袋員
13. baking products 烘烤用品	**16.** snack foods 點心食品	**19.** checker 收銀員	**22.** paper bag 紙袋
14. paper products 紙類用品	**17.** checkstand 結帳櫃台	**20.** line 排隊	**23.** plastic bag 塑膠袋

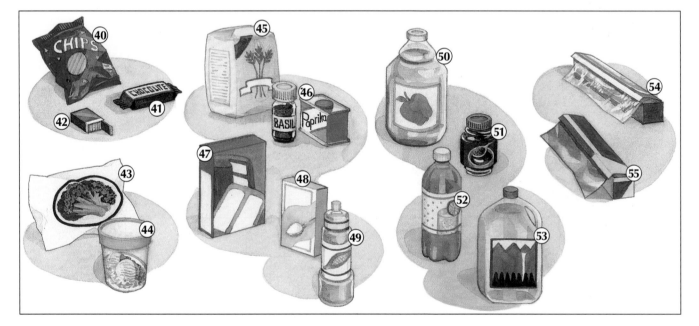

40. potato chips 洋芋片	**44.** ice cream 冰淇淋	**48.** sugar 糖	**52.** soda 汽水
41. candy bar 條狀糖果	**45.** flour 麵粉	**49.** oil 食用油	**53.** bottled water 瓶裝水
42. gum 口香糖	**46.** spices 香料	**50.** apple juice 蘋果汁	**54.** plastic wrap 保鮮膜
43. frozen vegetables 冷凍蔬菜	**47.** cake mix 調配好的蛋糕粉	**51.** instant coffee 即溶咖啡	**55.** aluminum foil 鋁箔紙

1. bottle
瓶子

2. jar
罐子

3. can
罐子

4. carton
紙盒

5. container
包

6. box
盒子

7. bag
袋子

8. package
包裝

9. six-pack
六罐裝

10. loaf
條

11. roll
捲

12. tube
管、條

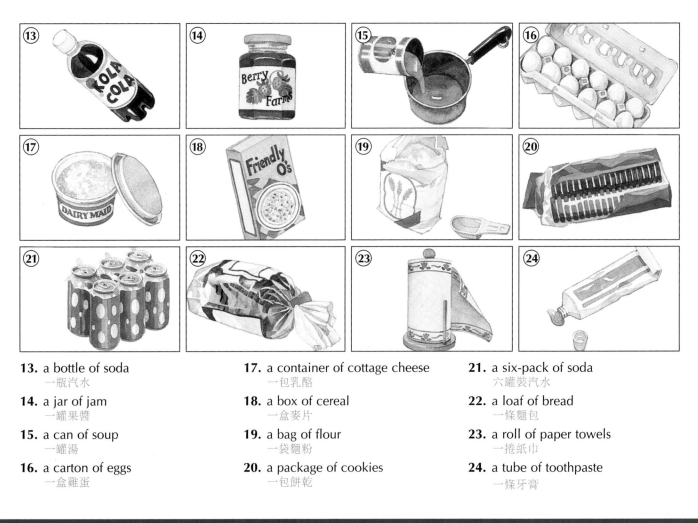

13. a bottle of soda
一瓶汽水

14. a jar of jam
一罐果醬

15. a can of soup
一罐湯

16. a carton of eggs
一盒雞蛋

17. a container of cottage cheese
一包乳酪

18. a box of cereal
一盒麥片

19. a bag of flour
一袋麵粉

20. a package of cookies
一包餅乾

21. a six-pack of soda
六罐裝汽水

22. a loaf of bread
一條麵包

23. a roll of paper towels
一捲紙巾

24. a tube of toothpaste
一條牙膏

Grammar point: *How much? How many?*

Some foods can be counted: *one apple, two apples.*

How many apples do you need? I need ***two*** apples.

Some foods cannot be counted, like liquids, grains, spices, or dairy foods. For these, count containers: *one box of rice, two boxes of rice.*

How much rice do you need? I need ***two boxes.***

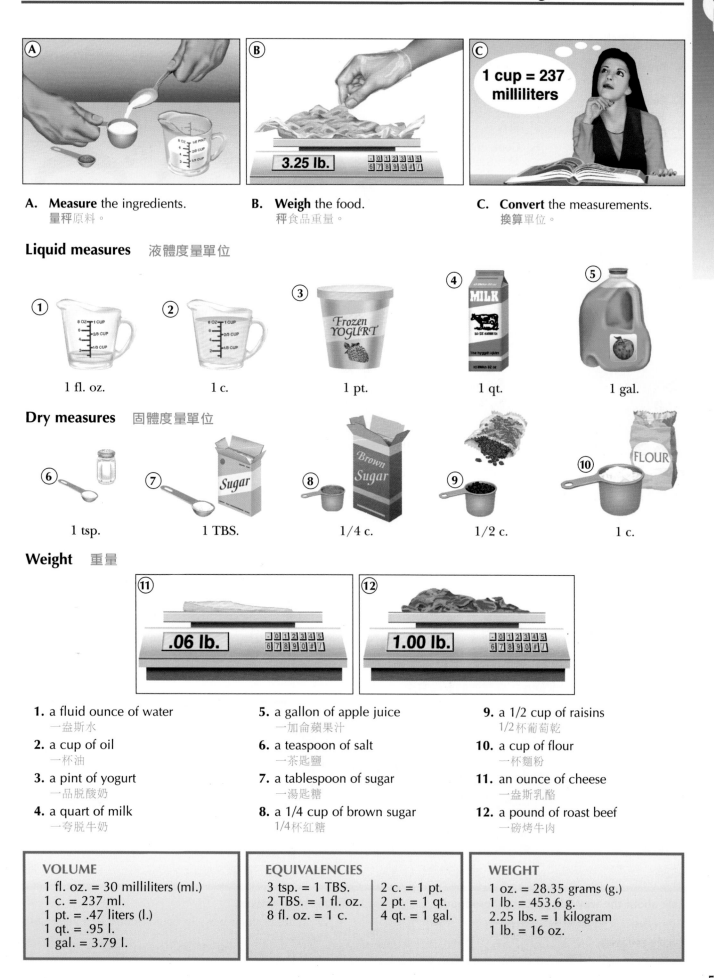

A. **Measure** the ingredients.
量秤原料。

B. **Weigh** the food.
秤食品重量。

C. **Convert** the measurements.
換算單位。

1 cup = 237 milliliters

Liquid measures 液體度量單位

1 fl. oz. 1 c. 1 pt. 1 qt. 1 gal.

Dry measures 固體度量單位

1 tsp. 1 TBS. 1/4 c. 1/2 c. 1 c.

Weight 重量

.06 lb. 1.00 lb.

1. a fluid ounce of water
一盎斯水

2. a cup of oil
一杯油

3. a pint of yogurt
一品脫酸奶

4. a quart of milk
一夸脫牛奶

5. a gallon of apple juice
一加侖蘋果汁

6. a teaspoon of salt
一茶匙鹽

7. a tablespoon of sugar
一湯匙糖

8. a 1/4 cup of brown sugar
1/4杯紅糖

9. a 1/2 cup of raisins
1/2杯葡萄乾

10. a cup of flour
一杯麵粉

11. an ounce of cheese
一盎斯乳酪

12. a pound of roast beef
一磅烤牛肉

VOLUME
1 fl. oz. = 30 milliliters (ml.)
1 c. = 237 ml.
1 pt. = .47 liters (l.)
1 qt. = .95 l.
1 gal. = 3.79 l.

EQUIVALENCIES	
3 tsp. = 1 TBS.	2 c. = 1 pt.
2 TBS. = 1 fl. oz.	2 pt. = 1 qt.
8 fl. oz. = 1 c.	4 qt. = 1 gal.

WEIGHT
1 oz. = 28.35 grams (g.)
1 lb. = 453.6 g.
2.25 lbs. = 1 kilogram
1 lb. = 16 oz.

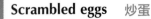

Scrambled eggs 炒蛋

A. Break 3 eggs.
打3個蛋。

B. Beat well.
攪拌均勻。

C. Grease the pan.
煎鍋放油。

D. Pour the eggs into the pan.
把蛋汁倒入鍋內。

E. Stir.
炒拌。

F. Cook until done.
煮到熟為止。

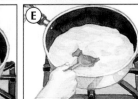

Vegetable casserole 烘焙蔬菜

G. Chop the onions.
切碎洋蔥。

H. Sauté the onions.
嫩煎洋蔥。

I. Steam the broccoli.
蒸綠花椰菜。

J. Grate the cheese.
乳酪銼成細條。

K. Mix the ingredients.
攪拌所有配料。

L. Bake at 350° for 45 minutes.
以350°烤45分鐘。

Chicken soup 雞湯

M. Cut up the chicken.
雞肉切塊。

N. Peel the carrots.
胡蘿蔔削皮。

O. Slice the carrots.
胡蘿蔔切片。

P. Boil the chicken.
煮雞肉。

Q. Add the vegetables.
加入蔬菜。

R. Simmer for 1 hour.
慢煮1小時。

Five ways to cook chicken 煮雞肉的五種方法

S. fry
煎炸

T. barbecue / grill
烤／炙

U. roast
烤焙

V. broil
烘烤

W. stir-fry
炒

Talk about the way you prepare these foods.

I *fry* eggs.

I *bake* potatoes.

Share your answers.

1. What are popular ways in your country to make rice? vegetables? meat?

2. What is your favorite way to cook chicken?

1. can opener
   開罐器
2. grater
   銼刀
3. plastic storage
   container
   塑料容器
4. steamer
   蒸鍋
5. frying pan
   煎鍋
6. pot
   鍋
7. ladle
   長柄勺子

8. double boiler
   雙層鍋
9. wooden spoon
   木勺
10. garlic press
    大蒜碾碎器
11. casserole dish
    焙盤
12. carving knife
    切刀
13. roasting pan
    烘烤盤
14. roasting rack
    烘烤架
15. vegetable peeler
    蔬菜削皮刀

16. paring knife
    削皮刀
17. colander
    濾鍋
18. kitchen timer
    炊煮計時器
19. spatula
    刮勺
20. eggbeater
    打蛋器
21. whisk
    攪拌器
22. strainer
    濾網
23. tongs
    夾鉗

24. lid
    鍋蓋
25. saucepan
    鍋
26. cake pan
    蛋糕盤
27. cookie sheet
    餅乾盤
28. pie pan
    派餅盤
29. pot holders
    拿鍋墊套
30. rolling pin
    麵棍
31. mixing bowl
    攪拌大碗

Talk about how to use the utensils.

You use a peeler to peel potatoes.

You use a pot to cook soup.

Use the new language.

Look at **Food Preparation**, page **58**.

Name the different utensils you see.

1. hamburger 漢堡	**8.** green salad 生菜沙拉	**15.** doughnut 甜甜圈	**22.** sugar substitute 代糖
2. french fries 炸薯條	**9.** taco 墨西哥塔可餅	**16.** salad bar 沙拉吧	**23.** ketchup 番茄醬
3. cheeseburger 起司漢堡	**10.** nachos 墨西哥黍片	**17.** lettuce 萵苣	**24.** mustard 芥末
4. soda 汽水	**11.** frozen yogurt 冷凍酸奶	**18.** salad dressing 沙拉醬	**25.** mayonnaise 美奶滋
5. iced tea 冰茶	**12.** milk shake 奶昔	**19.** booth 座位間	**26.** relish 作料
6. hot dog 熱狗	**13.** counter 櫃台	**20.** straw 吸管	**A.** eat 吃
7. pizza 披薩	**14.** muffin 鬆餅	**21.** sugar 白糖	**B.** drink 喝

More vocabulary

donut: doughnut (spelling variation)

condiments: relish, mustard, ketchup, mayonnaise, etc.

Share your answers.

1. What would you order at this restaurant?

2. Which fast foods are popular in your country?

3. How often do you eat fast food? Why?

1. scrambled eggs
   炒蛋

2. sausage
   香腸

3. toast
   烤麵包

4. waffles
   蛋奶烘餅

5. syrup
   糖漿

6. pancakes
   鬆餅

7. bacon
   醃豬肉

8. grilled cheese
   sandwich
   炙烤起司三明治

9. chef's salad
   廚師特製沙拉

10. soup of the day
    今日主湯

11. mashed potatoes
    洋芋泥

12. roast chicken
    烤雞

13. steak
    牛排

14. baked potato
    烤馬鈴薯

15. pasta
    麵食

16. garlic bread
    大蒜麵包

17. fried fish
    炸魚

18. rice pilaf
    米肉飯

19. cake
    蛋糕

20. pudding
    布丁

21. pie
    派

22. coffee
    咖啡

23. decaf coffee
    不含咖啡因的咖啡

24. tea
    茶

Practice ordering from the menu.

I'd like a grilled cheese sandwich and some soup.

I'll have the chef's salad and a cup of decaf coffee.

Use the new language.

Look at **Fruit**, page **50.**

Order a slice of pie using the different fruit flavors.

Please give me a slice of apple pie.

1. hostess
帶位人員

2. dining room
用餐室

3. menu
菜單

4. server/waiter
侍者／男侍者

5. patron/diner
用餐客人

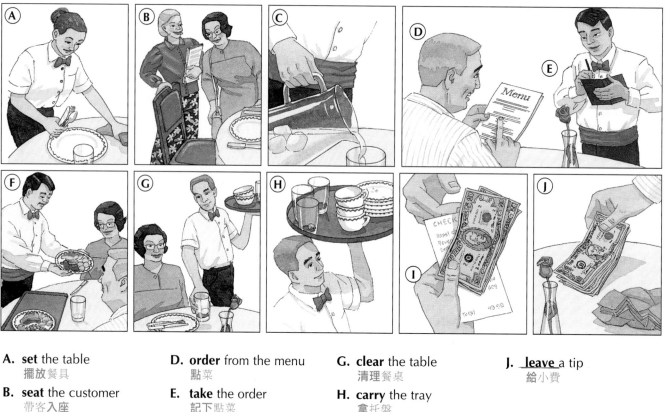

A. set the table
擺放餐具

B. seat the customer
帶客入座

C. pour the water
倒水

D. order from the menu
點菜

E. take the order
記下點菜

F. serve the meal
上菜

G. clear the table
清理餐桌

H. carry the tray
拿托盤

I. pay the check
付帳

J. leave a tip
給小費

More vocabulary

eat out: to go to a restaurant to eat

take out: to buy food at a restaurant and take it home
to eat

Practice giving commands.

Please <u>set the table</u>.

I'd like you to <u>clear the table</u>.

It's time to <u>serve the meal</u>.

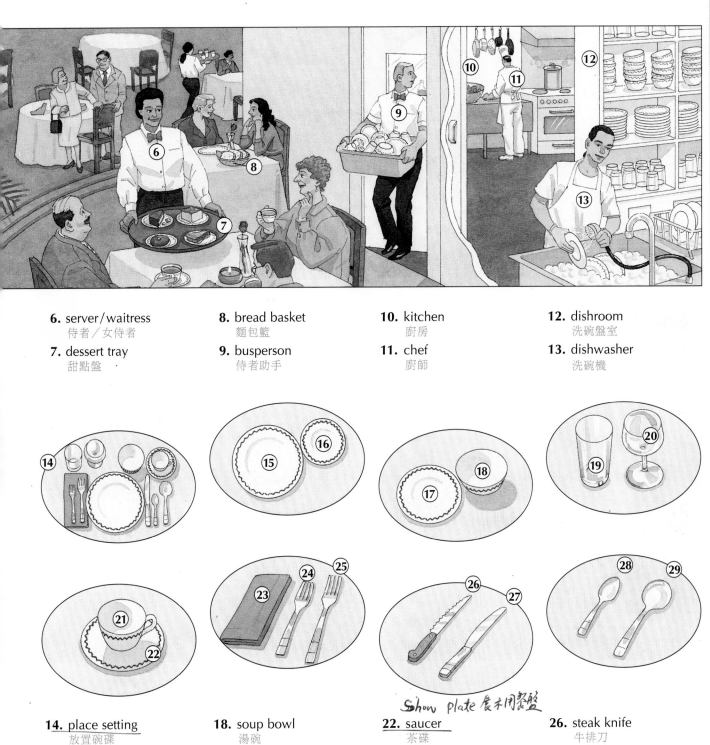

6. server／waitress
侍者／女侍者

7. dessert tray
甜點盤　·

8. bread basket
麵包籃

9. busperson
侍者助手

10. kitchen
廚房

11. chef
廚師

12. dishroom
洗碗盤室

13. dishwasher
洗碗機

Show plate 展未用餐盤

14. place setting
放置碗碟

15. dinner plate
主食盤

16. bread-and-butter plate
麵包、牛油盤

17. salad plate
沙拉盤

18. soup bowl
湯碗

19. water glass
水杯

20. wine glass
酒杯

21. cup
茶杯

22. saucer
茶碟

23. napkin
餐巾

24. salad fork
沙拉用叉

25. dinner fork
主食用叉

26. steak knife
牛排刀

27. knife
刀子

28. teaspoon
茶匙

29. soupspoon
湯匙

Talk about how you set the table in your home.

The glass is on the right.

The fork goes on the left.

The napkin is next to the plate.

Share your answers.

1. Do you know anyone who works in a restaurant? What does he or she do?

2. In your opinion, which restaurant jobs are hard? Why?

1. **three-piece suit**
   三件式西裝

2. **suit**
   西裝

3. **dress**
   洋裝

4. **shirt**
   襯衫

5. **jeans**
   牛仔褲

6. **sports coat**
   運動外套

7. **turtleneck**
   高領上衣

8. **slacks / pants**
   長褲

9. **blouse**
   女用上衣

10. **skirt**
    裙子

11. **pullover sweater**
    套頭毛衣

12. **T-shirt**
    T恤

13. **shorts**
    短褲

14. **sweatshirt**
    長袖運動衫

15. **sweatpants**
    運動褲

More vocabulary:

outfit: clothes that look nice together

When clothes are popular, they are **in fashion.**

Talk about what you're wearing today and what you wore yesterday.

I'm wearing a gray sweater, a red T-shirt, and blue jeans.

Yesterday I wore a green pullover sweater, a white shirt, and black slacks.

16. jumpsuit 連身衣	**21.** overalls 工人裝	**26.** sports shirt 運動襯衫
17. uniform 制服	**22.** tunic *corset.* 束腰外衣 */tjunik /*	**27.** cardigan sweater */kardzgən /* 羊毛衫
18. jumper 連衫裙	**23.** leggings 緊身褲 */legzy /*	**28.** tuxedo */tnk'sido /* 燕尾服
19. maternity dress 孕婦裝	**24.** vest 背心	**29.** evening gown 晚禮服
20. knit shirt 針織衫	**25.** split skirt 開叉裙	

Use the new language.

Look at **A Graduation**, pages **32–33**.

Name the clothes you see.

The man at the podium is wearing a suit.

Share your answers.

1. Which clothes in this picture are in fashion now?

2. Who is the best-dressed person in this line? Why?

3. What do you wear when you go to the movies?

1. hat 帽子	**5.** gloves 手套
2. overcoat 長大衣	**6.** cap 無邊帽
3. leather jacket 皮夾克	**7.** jacket 夾克
4. wool scarf/muffler 羊毛圍巾	

8. parka 風雪大衣	**12.** earmuffs 耳套
9. mittens 連指手套	**13.** down vest 鵝毛背心
10. ski cap 滑雪帽	**14.** ski mask 滑雪面罩
11. tights 緊身褲	**15.** down jacket 鵝毛夾克

16. umbrella 雨傘	**20.** trench coat 腰帶式雙排扣雨衣
17. raincoat 雨衣	**21.** sunglasses 太陽眼鏡
18. poncho 雨披	**22.** swimming trunks 游泳褲
19. rain boots 雨靴	**23.** strawhat 草帽

24. windbreaker 防風上衣	
25. cover-up 衣罩	
26. swimsuit/bathing suit 泳裝	
27. baseball cap 棒球帽	

Use the new language.

Look at **Weather**, page **10**.

Name the clothing for each weather condition.

Wear a jacket when it's windy.

Share your answers.

1. Which is better in the rain, an umbrella or a poncho?
2. Which is better in the cold, a parka or a down jacket?
3. Do you have more summer or winter clothes?

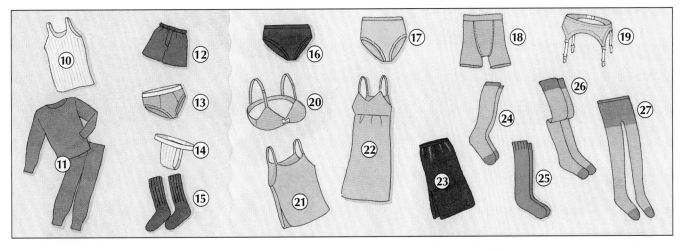

1. leotard
緊身衣

2. tank top
無袖短衫

3. bike shorts
運動短褲

4. pajamas
睡衣

5. nightgown
長袍

6. slippers
拖鞋

7. blanket sleeper
棉被衣

8. bathrobe
浴袍

9. nightshirt
男用長睡衣

10. undershirt
內衣

11. long underwear
內衣

12. boxer shorts
拳擊短褲

13. briefs
男用緊身內褲

14. athletic supporter / jockstrap
護襠

15. socks
襪子

16. (bikini) panties
（比基尼）三角褲

17. briefs / underpants
女用內褲

18. girdle
腰帶

19. garter belt
吊襪帶

20. bra
胸罩

21. camisole
內穿背心

22. full slip
長內衣

23. half slip
襯裙

24. knee-highs
及膝襪

25. kneesocks
短襪

26. stockings
長統襪

27. pantyhose
褲襪

More vocabulary

lingerie: underwear or sleepwear for women

loungewear: clothing (sometimes sleepwear) people wear around the home

Share your answers.

1. What do you wear when you exercise?

2. What kind of clothing do you wear for sleeping?

1. salesclerk
   銷售員
2. suspenders
   吊帶
3. shoe department
   售鞋部
4. silk scarves*
   絲巾
5. hats
   帽子

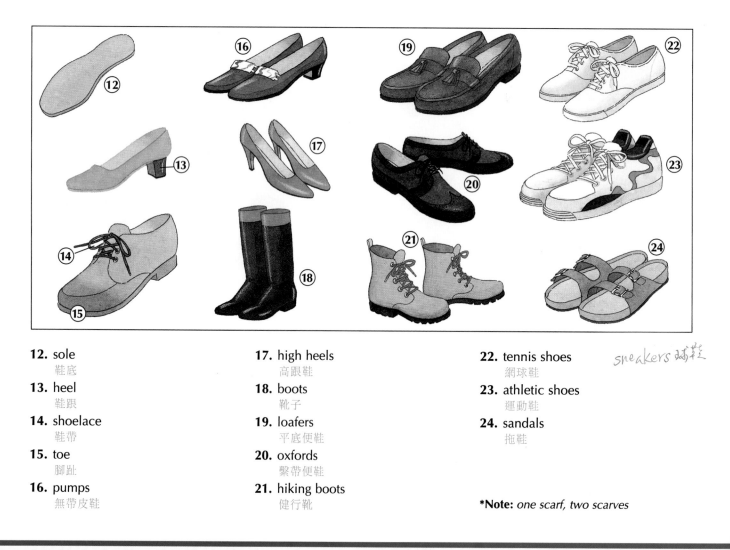

12. sole
    鞋底
13. heel
    鞋跟
14. shoelace
    鞋帶
15. toe
    腳趾
16. pumps
    無帶皮鞋

17. high heels
    高跟鞋
18. boots
    靴子
19. loafers
    平底便鞋
20. oxfords
    繫帶便鞋
21. hiking boots
    健行靴

22. tennis shoes
    網球鞋
23. athletic shoes
    運動鞋
24. sandals
    拖鞋

sneakers 球鞋

*Note: one scarf, two scarves

Talk about the shoes you're wearing today.

I'm wearing a pair of <u>white sandals</u>.

Practice asking a salesperson for help.

Could I try on these <u>sandals</u> in size <u>10</u>?

Do you have any <u>silk scarves</u>?

Where are <u>the hats</u>?

6. purses / handbags
皮包／手提袋

7. display case
展示櫃

8. jewelry
珠寶

9. necklaces
項鍊

10. ties
領帶

11. belts
皮帶

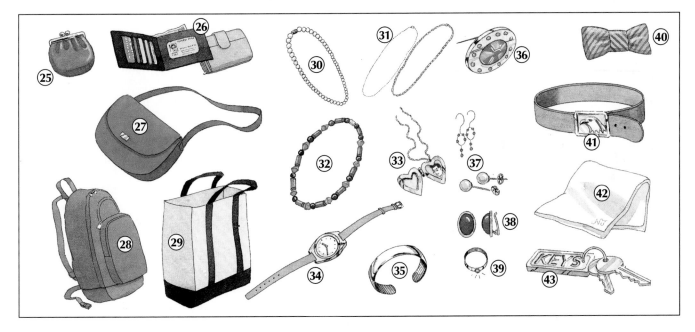

25. change purse
零錢包

26. wallet
皮夾

27. shoulder bag
肩背皮包

28. backpack / bookbag
背包／書包

29. tote bag
手提袋

30. string of pearls
一串珍珠

31. chain
鍊條

32. beads
珠鍊

33. locket
珠鍊小盒

34. (wrist)watch
（腕）錶

35. bracelet
手鐲

36. pin
別針

37. pierced earrings
穿洞耳環

38. clip-on earrings
夾耳耳環

39. ring
戒子

40. bow tie
領結

41. belt buckle
皮帶環扣

42. handkerchief
手帕

43. key chain
鑰匙圈

Share your answers.

1. Which of these accessories are usually worn by women? by men?

2. Which of these do you wear every day?

3. Which of these would you wear to a job interview? Why?

4. Which accessory would you like to receive as a present? Why?

Describing Clothes 描述衣服

Sizes 尺寸

1. extra small
特小號

2. small
小號

3. medium
中號

4. large
大號

5. extra large
特大號

Patterns 樣式

6. solid green
單綠色

7. striped
條紋

8. polka-dotted
圓點紋

9. plaid
方格紋

10. print
印花

11. checked
方格圖案

12. floral
花紋

13. paisley
華麗圖樣

Types of material 布料種類

14. wool sweater
羊毛衣

15. silk scarf
絲巾

16. cotton T-shirt
棉質T恤

17. linen jacket
亞麻夾克

18. leather boots
皮靴

19. nylon stockings*
尼龍襪

Problems 問題

20. too small
太小

21. too big
太大

22. stain
沾汙

23. rip / tear
扯破

24. broken zipper
拉鍊壞掉

25. missing button
缺扣子

*Note: Nylon, polyester, rayon, and plastic are synthetic materials.

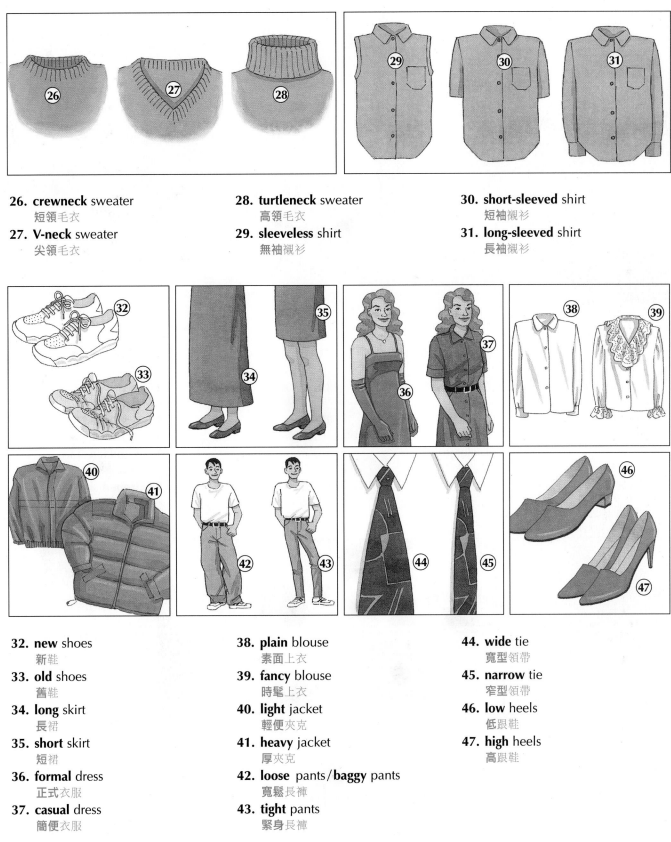

26. crewneck sweater
短領毛衣

27. V-neck sweater
尖領毛衣

28. turtleneck sweater
高領毛衣

29. sleeveless shirt
無袖襯衫

30. short-sleeved shirt
短袖襯衫

31. long-sleeved shirt
長袖襯衫

32. new shoes
新鞋

33. old shoes
舊鞋

34. long skirt
長裙

35. short skirt
短裙

36. formal dress
正式衣服

37. casual dress
簡便衣服

38. plain blouse
素面上衣

39. fancy blouse
時髦上衣

40. light jacket
輕便夾克

41. heavy jacket
厚夾克

42. loose pants/**baggy** pants
寬鬆長褲

43. tight pants
緊身長褲

44. wide tie
寬型領帶

45. narrow tie
窄型領帶

46. low heels
低跟鞋

47. high heels
高跟鞋

Talk about yourself.

I like <u>long-sleeved</u> shirts and <u>baggy</u> pants.

I like <u>short skirts</u> and <u>high heels</u>.

I usually wear <u>plain</u> clothes.

Share your answers.

1. What type of material do you usually wear in the summer? in the winter?

2. What patterns do you see around you?

3. Are you wearing casual or formal clothes?

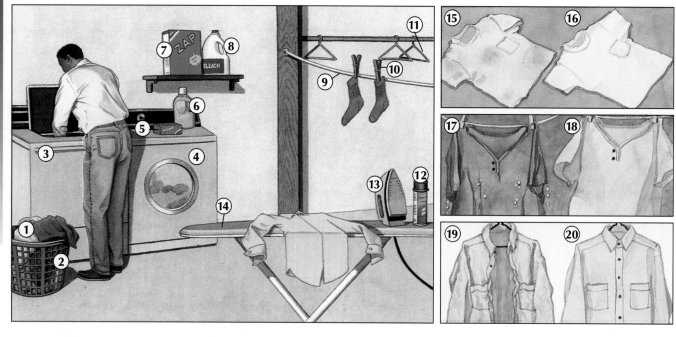

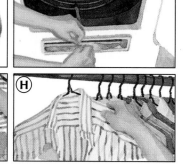

1. laundry
   換洗衣服

2. laundry basket
   衣籃

3. washer
   洗衣機

4. dryer
   烘乾機

5. dryer sheets
   烘乾紙

6. fabric softener
   衣服鬆軟劑

7. laundry detergent
   洗衣粉

8. bleach
   漂白粉

9. clothesline
   掛衣線

10. clothespin
    衣夾

11. hanger
    衣架

12. spray starch
    上漿

13. iron
    熨斗

14. ironing board
    燙衣板

15. **dirty** T-shirt
    髒T恤

16. **clean** T-shirt
    乾淨T恤

17. **wet** T-shirt
    溼T恤

18. **dry** T-shirt
    乾T恤

19. **wrinkled** shirt
    有綯褶的襯衫

20. **ironed** shirt
    燙平的襯衫

A. **Sort** the laundry.
   洗衣**分類**。

B. **Add** the detergent.
   放入洗衣粉。

C. **Load** the washer.
   把衣服**放入**洗衣機內。

D. **Clean** the lint trap.
   清理棉絨網。

E. **Unload** the dryer.
   把衣服從烘乾機內**拿出來**。

F. **Fold** the laundry.
   疊衣服。

G. **Iron** the clothes.
   燙熨衣服。

H. **Hang up** the clothes.
   掛衣服。

More vocabulary

dry cleaners: a business that cleans clothes using chemicals, not water and detergent

 wash in cold water only

no bleach

line dry

dry-clean only, do not wash

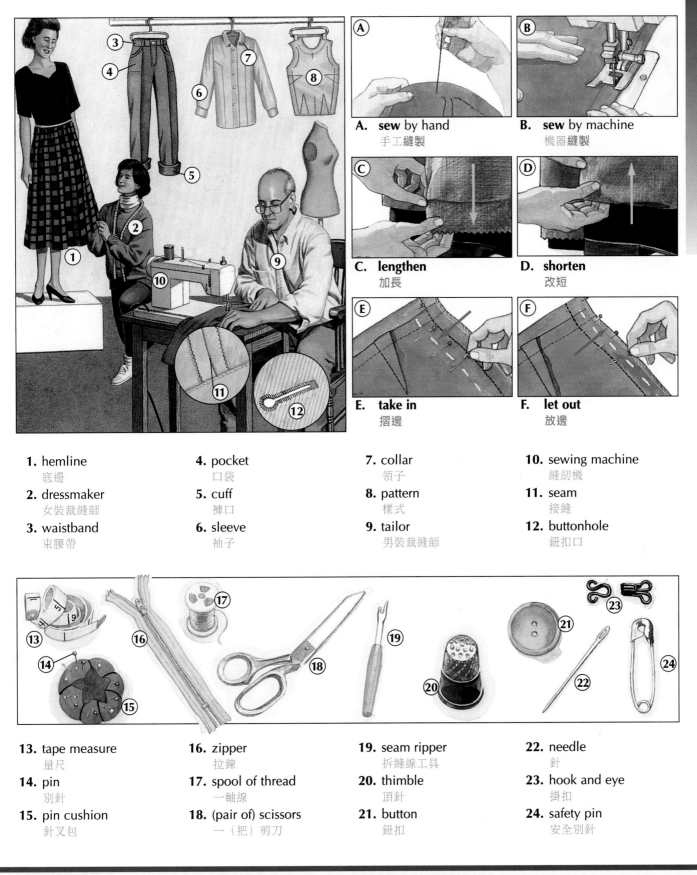

A. sew by hand
手工縫製

B. sew by machine
機器縫製

C. lengthen
加長

D. shorten
改短

E. take in
摺邊

F. let out
放邊

1. hemline
底邊

2. dressmaker
女裝裁縫師

3. waistband
束腰帶

4. pocket
口袋

5. cuff
褲口

6. sleeve
袖子

7. collar
領子

8. pattern
樣式

9. tailor
男裝裁縫師

10. sewing machine
縫紉機

11. seam
接縫

12. buttonhole
鈕扣口

13. tape measure
量尺

14. pin
別針

15. pin cushion
針叉包

16. zipper
拉鍊

17. spool of thread
一軸線

18. (pair of) scissors
一（把）剪刀

19. seam ripper
拆縫線工具

20. thimble
頂針

21. button
鈕扣

22. needle
針

23. hook and eye
掛扣

24. safety pin
安全別針

More vocabulary

pattern maker: a person who makes patterns

garment worker: a person who works in a clothing factory

fashion designer: a person who makes original clothes

Share your answers.

1. Do you know how to use a sewing machine?

2. Can you sew by hand?

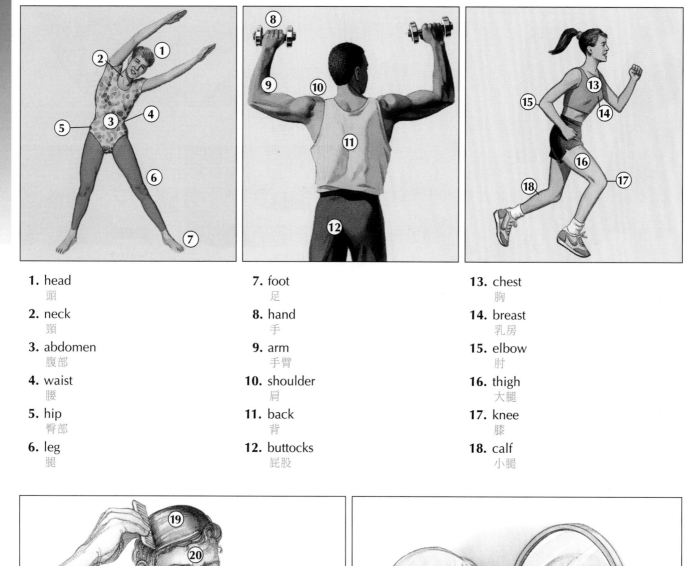

1. head
頭

2. neck
頸

3. abdomen
腹部

4. waist
腰

5. hip
臀部

6. leg
腿

7. foot
足

8. hand
手

9. arm
手臂

10. shoulder
肩

11. back
背

12. buttocks
屁股

13. chest
胸

14. breast
乳房

15. elbow
肘

16. thigh
大腿

17. knee
膝

18. calf
小腿

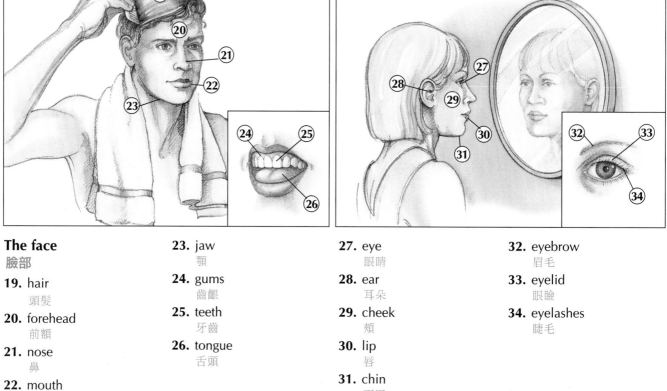

The face
臉部

19. hair
頭髮

20. forehead
前額

21. nose
鼻

22. mouth
嘴

23. jaw
顎

24. gums
齒齦

25. teeth
牙齒

26. tongue
舌頭

27. eye
眼睛

28. ear
耳朵

29. cheek
頰

30. lip
唇

31. chin
下巴

32. eyebrow
眉毛

33. eyelid
眼瞼

34. eyelashes
睫毛

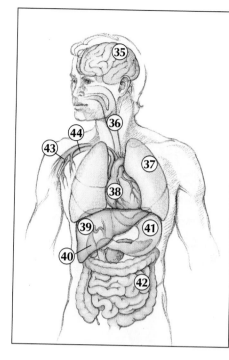

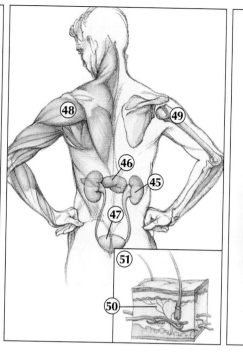

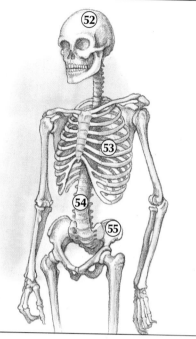

Inside the body
身體內部

35. brain
腦

36. throat
喉嚨

37. lung
肺

38. heart
心臟

39. liver
肝臟

40. gallbladder
膽囊

41. stomach
胃

42. intestines
腸

43. artery
動脈

44. vein
靜脈

45. kidney
腎

46. pancreas
胰

47. bladder
膀胱

48. muscle
肌肉

49. bone
骨

50. nerve
神經

51. skin
皮膚

The skeleton
骨骼

52. skull
顱骨

53. rib cage
肋骨

54. spinal column
脊椎骨

55. pelvis
骨盤

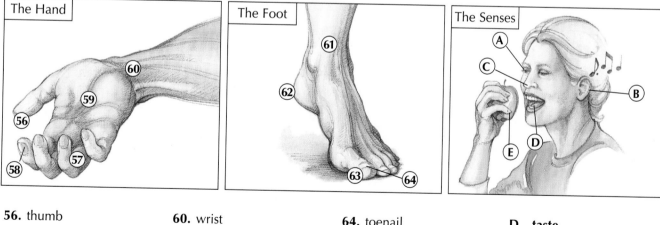

56. thumb
拇指

57. fingers
手指

58. fingernail
手指甲

59. palm
手掌

60. wrist
手腕

61. ankle
踝

62. heel
踵

63. toe
腳趾

64. toenail
腳趾甲

A. see
看

B. hear
聽

C. smell
聞

D. taste
嚐

E. touch
摸

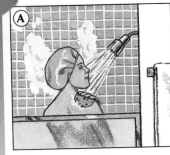

A. take a shower
洗淋浴

B. bathe / take a bath
洗澡

C. use deodorant
使用身體清香劑

D. put on sunscreen
擦防曬油

1. shower cap
   浴帽

2. soap
   香皂

3. bath powder / talcum powder
   爽身粉

4. deodorant
   身體清香劑

5. perfume / cologne
   香水／古龍水

6. sunscreen
   防曬油

7. body lotion
   身體乳液

8. moisturizer
   潤膚劑

 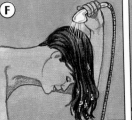    

E. wash…hair
洗…頭髮

F. rinse…hair
沖洗…頭髮

G. comb…hair
梳…頭髮

H. dry…hair
吹乾…頭髮

I. brush…hair
梳…頭髮

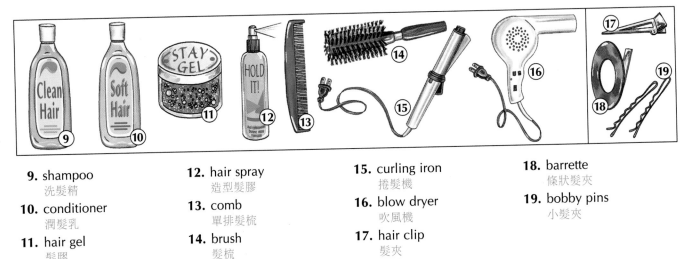

9. shampoo
   洗髮精

10. conditioner
    潤髮乳

11. hair gel
    髮膠

12. hair spray
    造型髮膠

13. comb
    單排髮梳

14. brush
    髮梳

15. curling iron
    捲髮機

16. blow dryer
    吹風機

17. hair clip
    髮夾

18. barrette
    條狀髮夾

19. bobby pins
    小髮夾

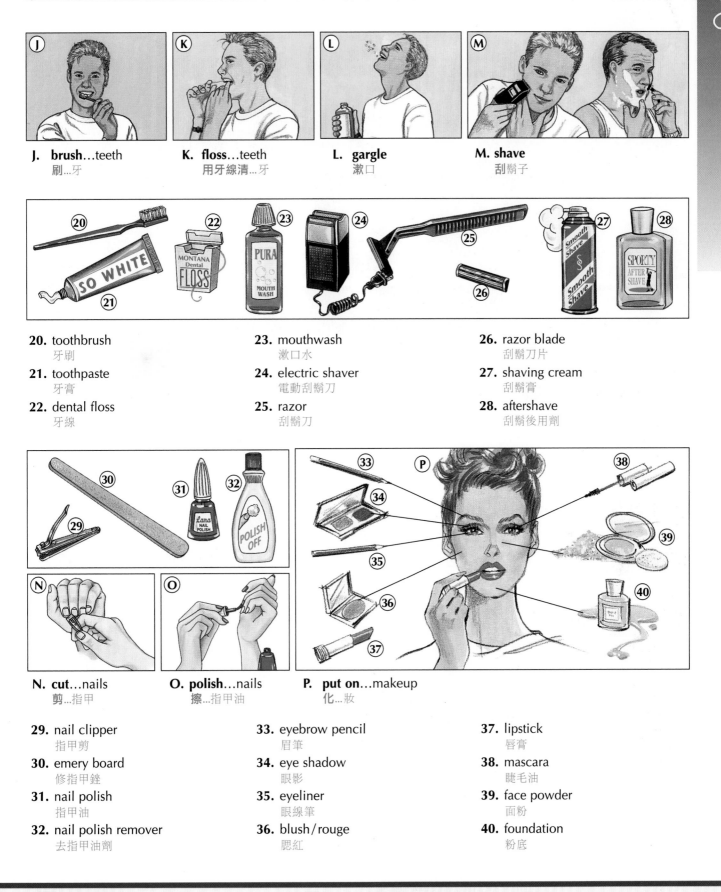

J. brush…teeth
刷…牙

K. floss…teeth
用牙線清…牙

L. gargle
漱口

M. shave
刮鬍子

20. toothbrush
牙刷

21. toothpaste
牙膏

22. dental floss
牙線

23. mouthwash
漱口水

24. electric shaver
電動刮鬍刀

25. razor
刮鬍刀

26. razor blade
刮鬍刀片

27. shaving cream
刮鬍膏

28. aftershave
刮鬍後用劑

N. cut…nails
剪…指甲

O. polish…nails
擦…指甲油

P. put on…makeup
化…妝

29. nail clipper
指甲剪

30. emery board
修指甲銼

31. nail polish
指甲油

32. nail polish remover
去指甲油劑

33. eyebrow pencil
眉筆

34. eye shadow
眼影

35. eyeliner
眼線筆

36. blush / rouge
腮紅

37. lipstick
唇膏

38. mascara
睫毛油

39. face powder
面粉

40. foundation
粉底

More vocabulary

A product without perfume or scent is **unscented.**

A product that is better for people with allergies is **hypoallergenic.**

Share your answers.

1. What is your morning routine if you stay home? if you go out?

2. Do women in your culture wear makeup? How old are they when they begin to use it?

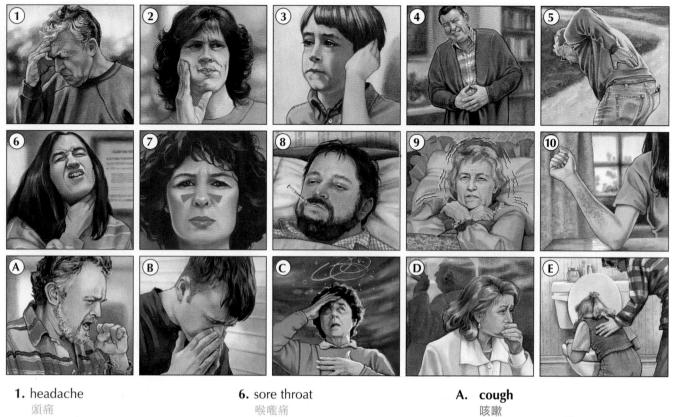

1. headache
頭痛

2. toothache
牙痛

3. earache
耳朵痛

4. stomachache
胃痛

5. backache
背痛

6. sore throat
喉嚨痛

7. nasal congestion
鼻塞

8. fever / temperature
發燒

9. chills
發冷

10. rash
疹子

A. **cough**
咳嗽

B. **sneeze**
打噴嚏

C. **feel** dizzy
感覺暈眩

D. **feel** nauseous
感覺噁心

E. **throw up / vomit**
嘔吐

  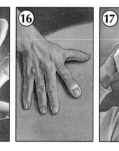 

11. insect bite
蚊蟲咬傷

12. bruise
瘀傷

13. cut
切傷

14. sunburn
曬傷

15. blister
水泡

16. **swollen** finger
手指紅腫

17. **bloody** nose
流鼻血

18. **sprained** ankle
腳踝扭傷

Use the new language.

Look at **Health Care**, pages **80–81.**

Tell what medication or treatment you would use for each health problem.

Share your answers.

1. For which problems would you go to a doctor? use medication? do nothing?

2. What do you do for a sunburn? for a headache?

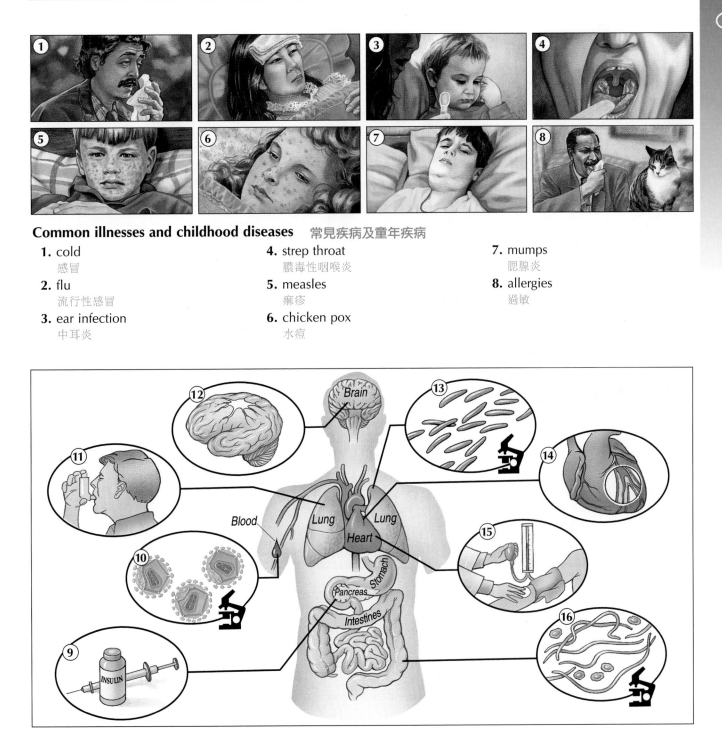

Common illnesses and childhood diseases 常見疾病及童年疾病

1. cold
   感冒
2. flu
   流行性感冒
3. ear infection
   中耳炎

4. strep throat
   膿毒性咽喉炎
5. measles
   痲疹
6. chicken pox
   水痘

7. mumps
   腮腺炎
8. allergies
   過敏

Medical conditions and serious diseases 病況及重病

9. diabetes
   糖尿病
10. HIV (human immunodeficiency virus)
    人類免疫系統不全病毒

11. asthma
    氣喘病
12. brain cancer
    腦癌
13. TB (tuberculosis)
    肺結核

14. heart disease
    心臟病
15. high blood pressure
    高血壓
16. intestinal parasites
    腸內寄生蟲

More vocabulary

AIDS (acquired immunodeficiency syndrome): a medical condition that results from contracting the HIV virus

influenza: flu

hypertension: high blood pressure

infectious disease: a disease that is spread through air or water

Share your answers.

What diseases on this page are infectious?

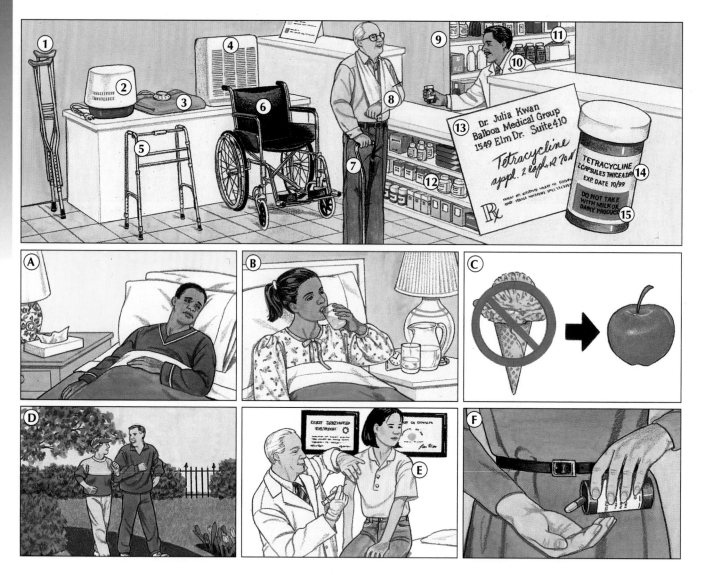

1. crutches
拐杖

2. humidifier
增溼機

3. heating pad
熱墊

4. air purifier
空氣淨化器

5. walker
行走扶架

6. wheelchair
輪椅

7. cane
手杖

8. sling
吊帶

9. pharmacy
藥房

10. pharmacist
藥劑師

11. prescription medication
處方藥

12. over-the-counter medication
架櫃上成藥

13. prescription
處方箋

14. prescription label
處方籤條

15. warning label
警告籤條

A. **Get** bed rest.
床上休息。

B. **Drink** fluids.
飲用液體。

C. **Change** your diet.
改變飲食。

D. **Exercise.**
運動。

E. **Get** an injection.
注射。

F. **Take** medicine.
吃藥。

More vocabulary

dosage: how much medicine you take and how many times a day you take it

expiration date: the last day the medicine can be used

treatment: something you do to get better

Staying in bed, drinking fluids, getting physical therapy are treatments.

An injection that stops a person from getting a serious disease is called **an immunization** or **a vaccination.**

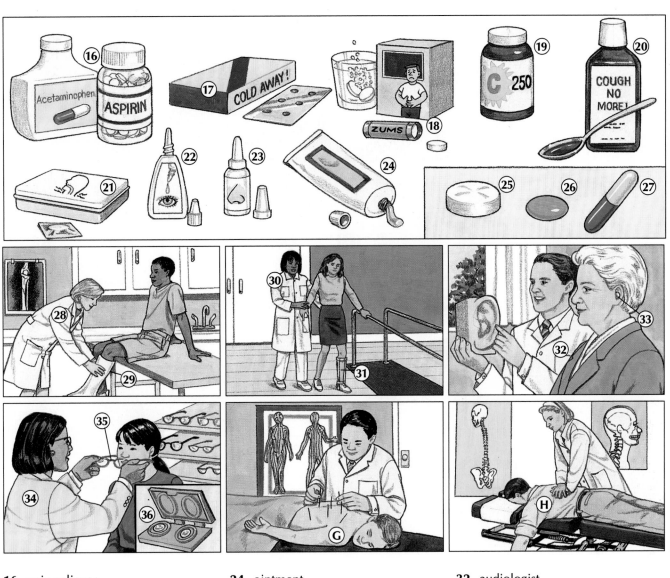

16. pain reliever
止痛藥

17. cold tablets
感冒錠

18. antacid
制酸藥

19. vitamins
維他命

20. cough syrup
止咳糖漿

21. throat lozenges
喉片

22. eyedrops
眼藥水

23. nasal spray
噴鼻劑

24. ointment
藥膏

25. tablet
藥錠

26. pill
藥丸

27. capsule
膠囊

28. orthopedist
整形外科醫師

29. cast
石膏

30. physical therapist
物理治療師

31. brace
肢體矯正器

32. audiologist
聽覺檢查師

33. hearing aid
助聽器

34. optometrist
驗光師

35. (eye)glasses
（眼）鏡

36. contact lenses
隱形鏡片

G. **Get** acupuncture.
針灸治療。

H. **Go** to a chiropractor.
脊椎治療。

Share your answers.

1. What's the best treatment for a headache? a sore throat? a stomachache? a fever?

2. Do you think vitamins are important? Why or why not?

3. What treatments are popular in your culture?

A. **be injured / be hurt**
受傷

B. **be** unconscious
失去知覺

C. **be** in shock
休克

D. **have** a heart attack
心臟病突發

E. **have** an allergic reaction
發生過敏反應

F. **get** an electric shock
受到電擊

G. **get** frostbite
凍傷

H. **burn** (your)self
灼傷（你）自己

I. **drown**
溺水

J. **swallow** poison
吞食有毒物質

K. **overdose** on drugs
用藥過量

L. **choke**
噎塞

M. **bleed**
流血

N. **can't breathe**
不能呼吸

O. **fall**
跌倒

P. **break** a bone
骨折

Grammar point: past tense

burn	—	burned	choke	—	choked	bleed	—	bled
drown	—	drowned	be	—	was, were	can't	—	couldn't
swallow	—	swallowed	have	—	had	fall	—	fell
overdose	—	overdosed	get	—	got	break	—	broke

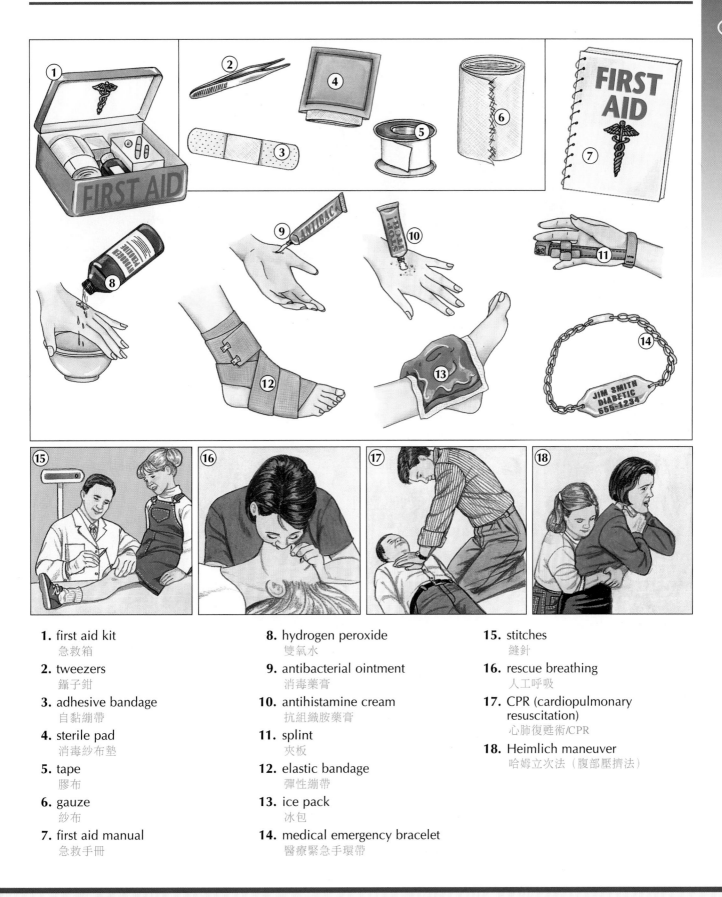

1. **first aid kit**
   急救箱

2. **tweezers**
   鑷子鉗

3. **adhesive bandage**
   自黏繃帶

4. **sterile pad**
   消毒紗布墊

5. **tape**
   膠布

6. **gauze**
   紗布

7. **first aid manual**
   急救手冊

8. **hydrogen peroxide**
   雙氧水

9. **antibacterial ointment**
   消毒藥膏

10. **antihistamine cream**
    抗組織胺藥膏

11. **splint**
    夾板

12. **elastic bandage**
    彈性繃帶

13. **ice pack**
    冰包

14. **medical emergency bracelet**
    醫療緊急手環帶

15. **stitches**
    縫針

16. **rescue breathing**
    人工呼吸

17. **CPR (cardiopulmonary resuscitation)**
    心肺復甦術/CPR

18. **Heimlich maneuver**
    哈姆立次法（腹部擠擠法）

Important Note: Only people who are properly trained should give stitches or do CPR.

Share your answers.

1. Do you have a First Aid kit in your home? Where can you buy one?

2. When do you use hydrogen peroxide? an elastic support bandage? antihistamine cream?

3. Do you know first aid? Where did you learn it?

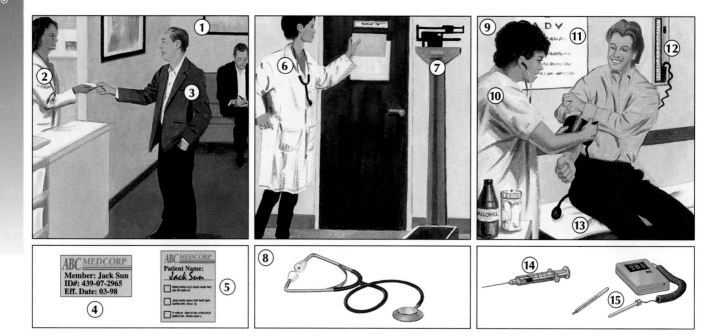

Medical clinic 醫療診所

1. waiting room
候診室

2. receptionist
櫃台人員

3. patient
病人

4. insurance card
醫療保險卡

5. insurance form
保險表格

6. doctor
醫生

7. scale
體重器

8. stethoscope
聽診器

9. examining room
診斷室

10. nurse
護士

11. eye chart
視力檢查表

12. blood pressure gauge
血壓計

13. examination table
診斷床

14. syringe
注射器

15. thermometer
溫度計

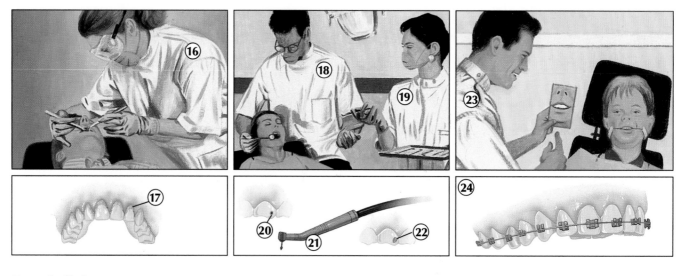

Dental clinic 牙科診所

16. dental hygienist
口腔衛生師

17. tartar
牙垢

18. dentist
牙醫師

19. dental assistant
牙醫助理

20. cavity
蛀牙

21. drill
牙鑽

22. filling
補牙粉

23. orthodontist
矯正牙醫師

24. braces
牙套

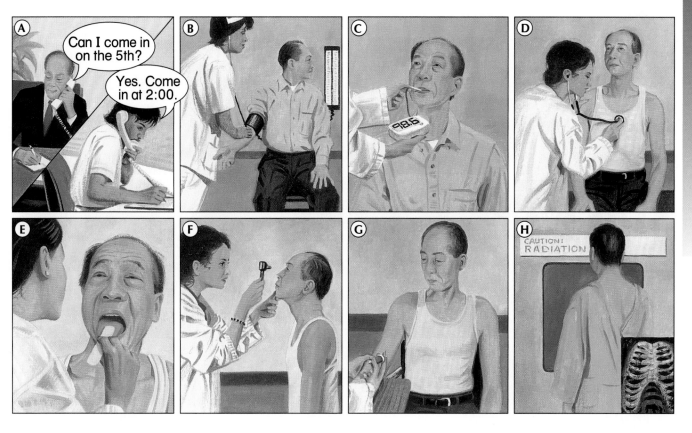

A. **make** an appointment
約診

B. **check**…blood pressure
量…血壓

C. **take**…temperature
量…溫度

D. **listen** to…heart
聽…心跳

E. **look** in…throat
檢查…喉嚨

F. **examine**…eyes
檢查…眼睛

G. **draw**…blood
抽…血

H. **get** an X ray
照…X光

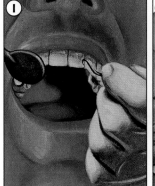 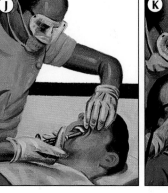 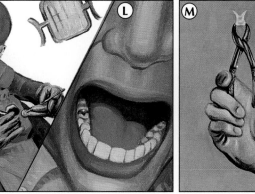 

I. **clean**…teeth
清潔…牙齒

J. **give**…a shot of anesthetic
打…麻醉藥

K. **drill** a tooth
鑽牙齒

L. **fill** a cavity
補牙

M. **pull** a tooth
拔牙

More vocabulary

get a checkup: to go for a medical exam

extract a tooth: to pull out a tooth

Share your answers.

1. What is the average cost of a medical exam in your area?

2. Some people are nervous at the dentist's office. What can they do to relax?

Hospital staff 醫院職員

1. obstetrician
產科醫師

2. internist
內科醫師

3. cardiologist
心臟科醫師

4. pediatrician
小兒科醫師

5. radiologist
放射科醫師

6. psychiatrist
心理醫師

7. ophthalmologist
眼科醫師

8. X-ray technician
X光醫技員

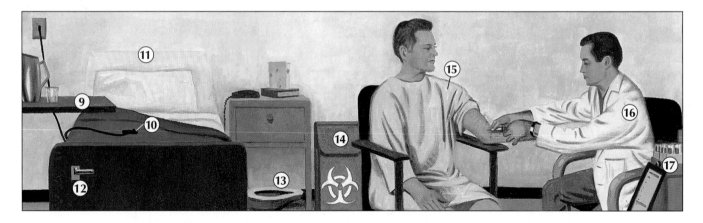

Patient's room 病房

9. bed table
病床邊桌

10. call button
呼叫鈕

11. hospital bed
病床

12. bed control
病床控制

13. bedpan
便盆

14. medical waste disposal
醫療用品廢棄桶

15. hospital gown
病人穿著用袍

16. lab technician
化驗室醫技人員

17. blood work/blood test
驗血

More vocabulary

nurse practitioner: a nurse licensed to give medical exams

specialist: a doctor who only treats specific medical problems

gynecologist: a specialist who examines and treats women

nurse midwife: a nurse practitioner who examines pregnant women and delivers babies

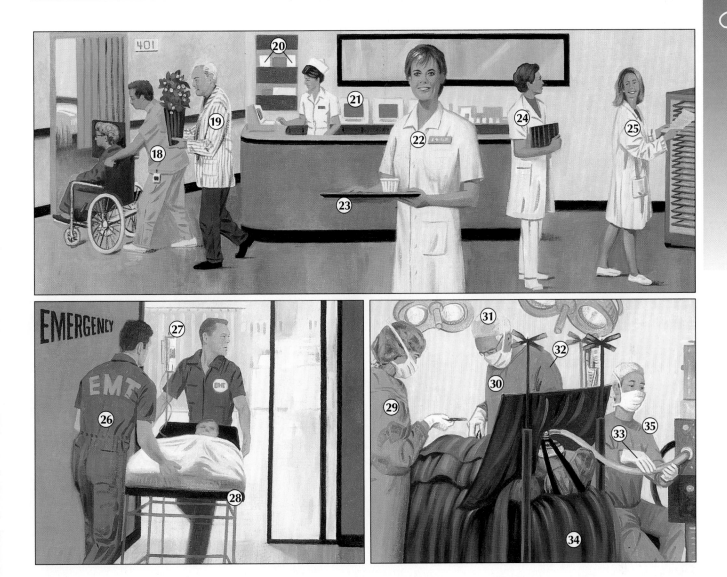

Nurse's station
護士站

18. orderly
勤雜工

19. volunteer
義工

20. medical charts
病歷表

21. vital signs monitor
病人生理狀況監視器

22. RN (registered nurse)
註冊護士

23. medication tray
藥品托盤

24. LPN (licensed practical nurse)/
LVN (licensed vocational nurse)
有照職業護士

25. dietician
營養師

Emergency room
急診室

26. emergency medical technician (EMT)
急診醫療技術人員

27. IV (intravenous drip)
點滴

28. stretcher / gurney
擔架車

Operating room
手術室

29. surgical nurse
外科護士

30. surgeon
外科醫生

31. surgical cap
手術帽

32. surgical gown
手術衣

33. latex gloves
橡膠手套

34. operating table
手術台

35. anesthesiologist
麻醉師

Practice asking for the hospital staff.

Please get the nurse. I have a question for her.
Where's the anesthesiologist? I need to talk to her.
I'm looking for the lab technician. Have you seen him?

Share your answers.

1. Have you ever been to an emergency room? Who helped you?

2. Have you ever been in the hospital? How long did you stay?

1. fire station
   消防隊

2. coffee shop
   咖啡店

3. bank
   銀行

4. car dealership
   汽車經銷商

5. hotel
   旅館

6. church
   教堂

7. hospital
   醫院

8. park
   公園

9. synagogue /ˈsɪnəgɒg/
   猶太教堂

10. theater
    劇院

11. movie theater
    電影院

12. gas station
    加油站

13. furniture store
    傢具店

14. hardware store
    五金店

15. barber shop
    理髮店

More vocabulary

skyscraper: a very tall office building

downtown/city center: the area in a city with the
city hall, courts, and businesses

Practice giving your destination.

I'm going to go downtown.

I have to go to the post office.

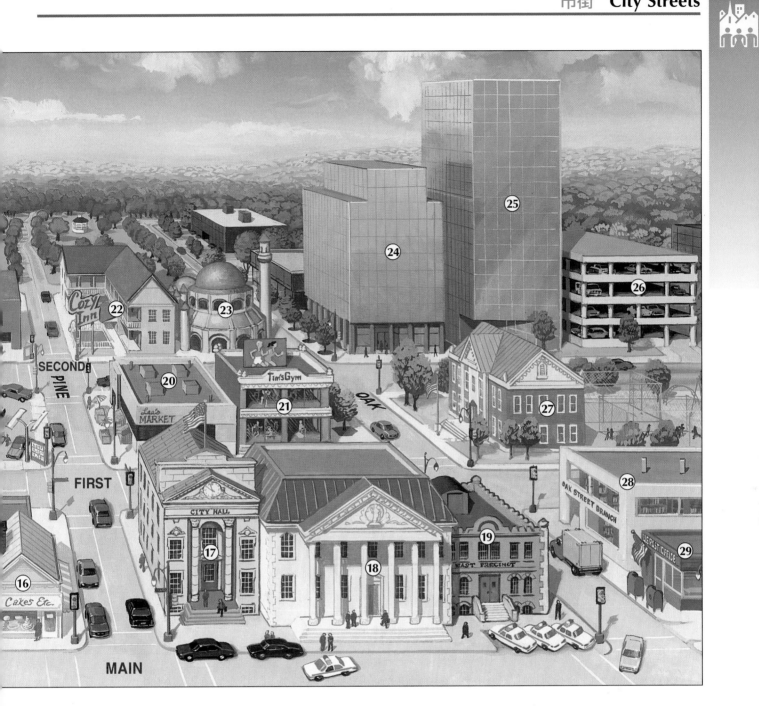

16. bakery
麵包店

17. city hall
市政廳

18. courthouse
法院

19. police station
警察局

20. market
市場

21. health club
健身中心

22. motel
汽車旅館

23. mosque /mask/
清真寺

24. office building
辦公大樓

25. high-rise building
摩天大樓

26. parking garage
停車場

27. school
學校

28. library
圖書館

29. post office
郵局

upscale 上等級旅店.

Practice asking for and giving the locations of buildings.

Where's the post office?

  It's on Oak Street.

Share your answers.

1. Which of the places in this picture do you go to every week?

2. Is it good to live in a city? Why or why not?

3. What famous cities do you know?

1. Laundromat
自助洗衣店

2. drugstore/pharmacy
雜貨店／藥房

3. convenience store
便利商店

4. photo shop
照相館

5. parking space
停車位

6. traffic light
交通燈號

7. pedestrian /pə'dɛstrɪən/
行人

8. crosswalk
行人穿越道

9. street
街、馬路

10. curb
路邊石

11. newsstand
報攤

12. mailbox
信箱

13. drive-thru window
直駛購物窗口

14. fast food restaurant
速食餐館

15. bus
汽車

A. **cross** the street
穿越馬路

B. **wait** for the light
等待交通燈號

C. **drive** a car
開車

More vocabulary

neighborhood: the area close to your home

do errands: to make a short trip from your home to buy or pick up something

Talk about where to buy things.

You can buy <u>newspapers</u> at <u>a newsstand</u>.

You can buy <u>donuts</u> at <u>a donut shop</u>.

You can buy <u>food</u> at <u>a convenience store</u>.

16. bus stop
公車站

17. corner
街角

18. parking meter
停車計費表

19. motorcycle
摩托車

20. donut shop
甜甜圈餅店

21. public telephone
公用電話

22. copy center / print shop
複印／印刷店

23. streetlight
街燈

24. dry cleaners
乾洗店

25. nail salon
修指甲店

26. sidewalk
人行道

27. garbage truck
垃圾車

28. fire hydrant /ˈhaɪdrɛ/
消防栓

29. sign
標誌

30. street vendor
小販

31. cart
手推車

D. **park** the car
停車

E. **ride** a bicycle
騎自行車

Share your answers.

1. Do you like to do errands?

2. Do you always like to go to the same stores?

3. Which businesses in the picture are also in your neighborhood?

4. Do you know someone who has a small business? What kind?

5. What things can you buy from a street vendor?

91

1. music store
   音樂店
2. jewelry store
   珠寶店
3. candy store
   糖果店
4. bookstore
   書店
5. toy store
   玩具店
6. pet store
   寵物店
7. card store
   卡片店
8. optician
   眼鏡店
9. travel agency
   旅行社
10. shoe store
    鞋店
11. fountain
    噴水池
12. florist
    花店

More vocabulary

beauty shop: hair salon

men's store: a store that sells men's clothing

dress shop: a store that sells women's clothing

Talk about where you want to shop in this mall.

Let's go to the card store.

I need to buy a card for Maggie's birthday.

13. department store
百貨公司

14. food court
餐飲區

15. video store
錄影帶店

16. hair salon
美容院

17. maternity shop
孕婦用品店

18. electronics store
電器用品店

19. directory + assistance 查詢站
地點標示圖

20. ice cream stand
冰淇淋攤子
swirl twist

21. escalator
自動扶梯

22. information booth
詢問處 lost and found.

Practice asking for and giving the location of different shops.

Where's the maternity shop?

It's on the first floor, next to the hair salon.

Share your answers.

1. Do you like shopping malls? Why or why not?

2. Some people don't go to the mall to shop.
Name some other things you can do in a mall.

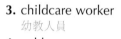

1. parent
父母

2. stroller
幼兒手推車

3. childcare worker
幼教人員

4. cubby
小壁櫥

5. toys
玩具

6. rocking chair
搖椅

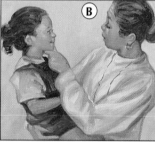

A. **drop off**
送孩子到托兒所

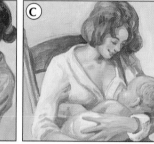

B. **hold**
抱

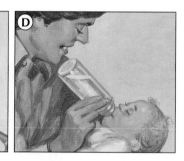

C. **nurse**
哺乳

D. **feed**
餵食

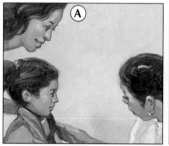

E. **change** diapers
換尿布

F. **read** a story
讀故事

G. **pick up**
接孩子

H. **rock**
搖

I. **tie** shoes
繫鞋帶

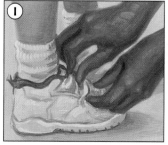

J. **dress**
穿衣服

K. **play**
玩

L. **take** a nap
睡午覺

7. high chair
兒童高座椅

8. bib
圍兜

9. changing table
換尿布桌台

10. potty seat
孩童便盆

11. playpen
幼兒圍欄床

12. walker
學步車

13. car safety seat
汽車安全座椅

14. baby carrier
嬰兒提籃

15. baby backpack
嬰兒背帶

16. carriage
嬰兒車

17. wipes
濕巾

18. baby powder
嬰兒爽身粉

19. disinfectant
殺菌劑

20. disposable diapers
紙尿布

21. cloth diapers
布尿布

22. diaper pins
尿布別針

23. diaper pail
尿布桶

24. training pants
訓練兒童如廁尿布褲

25. formula
奶粉

26. bottle
奶瓶

27. nipple
奶嘴

28. baby food
嬰兒食品

29. pacifier
嬰兒奶嘴

30. teething ring
磨牙圈

31. rattle
響環

1. envelope
   信封
2. letter
   信紙
3. postcard
   明信片
4. greeting card
   問候卡
5. package
   包裹

6. letter carrier
   郵差
7. return address
   寄信人地址
8. mailing address
   收信人地址
9. postmark
   郵戳
10. stamp / postage
    郵票／郵資

11. certified mail
    掛號信
12. priority mail
    快信
13. air letter / aerogramme
    航空信
14. ground post /
    parcel post
    陸運／包裹郵件
15. Express Mail /
    overnight mail
    特快信／次日即遞信件

A. **address** a postcard
   明信片上寫上地址
B. **send** it／**mail** it
   送／寄信

C. **deliver** it
   遞送信件
D. **receive** it
   接收信件

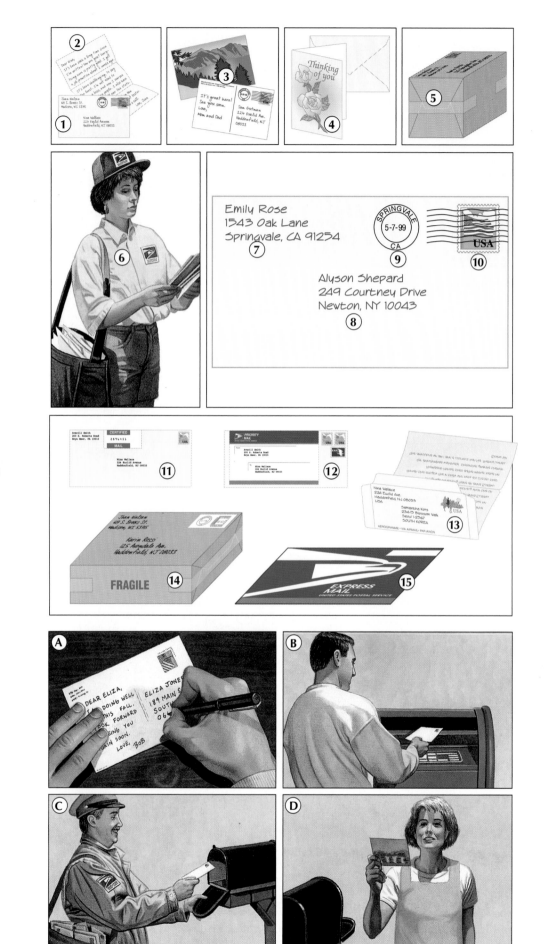

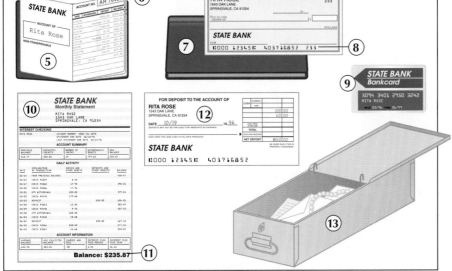

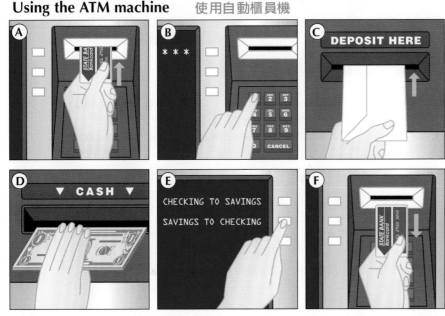

1. teller
   出納員
2. vault
   貴重品保管室
3. ATM (automated teller machine)
   自動櫃員機
4. security guard
   警衛

5. passbook'
   存摺
6. savings account number
   儲蓄帳戶號碼
7. checkbook
   支票簿
8. checking account number
   支票帳戶號碼
9. ATM card
   自動存提款卡
10. monthly statement
    每月帳戶往來明細表
11. balance
    餘額
12. deposit slip
    存款單
13. safe-deposit box
    出租保險箱

Using the ATM machine   使用自動櫃員機

A. **Insert** your ATM card.
   插入自動存提款卡。
B. **Enter** your PIN number.*
   輸入個人密碼。
C. **Make** a deposit.
   存款。

D. **Withdraw** cash.
   提款。
E. **Transfer** funds.
   轉帳。
F. **Remove** your ATM card.
   取出自動存提款卡。

*PIN: personal identification number

More vocabulary

overdrawn account: When there is not enough money in an account to pay a check, we say the account is overdrawn.

Share your answers.

1. Do you use a bank?
2. Do you use an ATM card?
3. Name some things you can put in a safe-deposit box.

1. reference librarian 圖書館員	**7.** magazine 雜誌	**13.** videocassette 錄影帶	**19.** library card 圖書館卡
2. reference desk 查閱台	**8.** newspaper 報紙	**14.** CD (compact disc) 光碟片	**20.** library book 圖書館的書
3. atlas 地圖	**9.** online catalog 電腦線上目錄	**15.** record n. 唱片	**21.** title 書名
4. microfilm reader 縮影膠片放映機	**10.** card catalog 書卡目錄	**16.** checkout desk 出借登記處	**22.** author 作者
5. microfilm 縮影膠片	**11.** media section 媒體室	**17.** library clerk 圖書館職員	
6. periodical section 期刊室	**12.** audiocassette 錄音帶	**18.** encyclopedia [ɪn, saɪkləˈpɪdtə] 百科全書	

More vocabulary

check a book out: to borrow a book from the library

nonfiction: real information, history or true stories

fiction: stories from the author's imagination

Share your answers.

1. Do you have a library card?

2. Do you prefer to buy books or borrow them from the library?

A. **arrest** a suspect
逮捕嫌犯
1. police officer
警察
2. handcuffs
手銬

B. **hire** a lawyer / **hire** an attorney
聘雇律師
3. guard
警衛
4. defense attorney
辯方律師

C. **appear** in court
出庭
5. defendant
被告
6. judge
法官

D. **stand trial**
開庭審判
7. courtroom
法庭

8. jury
陪審團
9. evidence
證據

10. prosecuting attorney
檢察官（控方律師）
11. witness
證人

12. court reporter
法院書記員
13. bailiff
庭警

E. **give** the verdict*
判決

F. **sentence** the defendant
宣判被告刑罰

G. **go** to jail / **go** to prison
坐牢
14. convict
定罪

H. **be released**
釋放

*Note: There are two possible verdicts, "guilty" and "not guilty."

Share your answers.

1. What are some differences between the legal system in the United States and the one in your country?

2. Do you want to be on a jury? Why or why not?

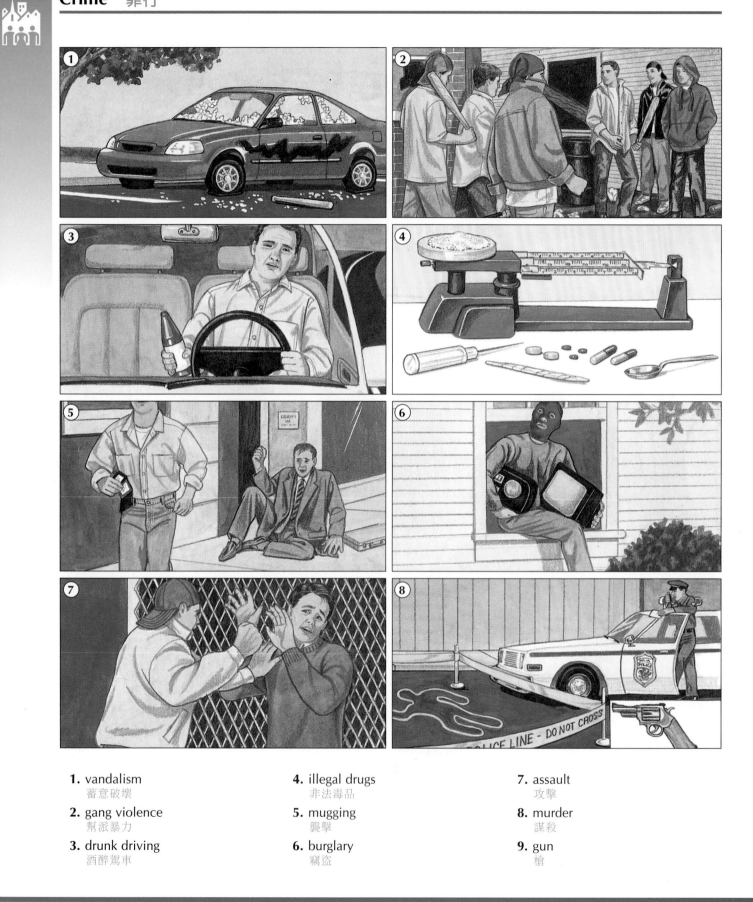

1. vandalism
   蓄意破壞

2. gang violence
   幫派暴力

3. drunk driving
   酒醉駕車

4. illegal drugs
   非法毒品

5. mugging
   襲擊

6. burglary
   竊盜

7. assault
   攻擊

8. murder
   謀殺

9. gun
   槍

More vocabulary

commit a crime: to do something illegal

criminal: someone who commits a crime

victim: someone who is hurt or killed by someone else

Share your answers.

1. Is there too much crime on TV? in the movies?

2. Do you think people become criminals from watching crime on TV?

A. **Walk** with a friend.
　與朋友**並行**。

B. **Stay** on well-lit streets.
　停留在光線良好的街上。

C. **Hold** your purse close to your body.
　把皮包**拿住**靠近身體。

D. **Protect** your wallet.
　保護皮夾。

E. **Lock** your doors.
　鎖門。

F. **Don't open** your door to strangers.
　不要給陌生人**開門**。

G. **Don't drink** and **drive**.
　切勿酒後駕車。

H. **Report** crimes to the police.
　報警處理犯罪事件。

More vocabulary

Neighborhood Watch: a group of neighbors who watch for criminals in their neighborhood

designated drivers: people who don't drink alcoholic beverages so that they can drive drinkers home

Share your answers.

1. Do you feel safe in your neighborhood?

2. Look at the pictures. Which of these things do you do?

3. What other things do you do to stay safe?

1. lost child
孩子走失

2. car accident
車禍

3. airplane crash
墜機

4. explosion
爆炸

5. earthquake
地震

6. mudslide
坍方

7. fire
火災

8. firefighter
救火員

9. fire truck
消防車

Practice reporting a fire.

This is <u>Lisa Broad</u>. There is a fire.

The address is <u>323 Oak Street</u>.

Please send someone quickly.

Share your answers.

1. Can you give directions to your home if there is a fire?

2. What information do you give to the other driver if you are in a car accident?

10. drought
乾旱

11. blizzard
暴風雪

12. hurricane
颶風

13. tornado
龍捲風

14. volcanic eruption
火山爆發

15. tidal wave
潮浪

16. flood
水災

17. search and rescue team
尋找援救隊

Share your answers.

1. Which disasters are common in your area? Which never happen?

2. What can you do to prepare for emergencies?

3. Do you have emergency numbers near your telephone?

4. Which organizations will help you in an emergency?

1. bus stop
   公車站
2. route
   路線
3. schedule
   行車時間表
4. bus
   公車
5. fare
   車資
6. transfer
   換車

7. passenger
   乘客
8. bus driver
   公車司機
9. subway
   地鐵
10. track
    鐵軌
11. token
    地鐵代用幣
12. fare card
    車票卡

13. train station
    火車站
14. ticket
    車票
15. platform
    月台
16. conductor
    車掌
17. train
    火車
18. taxi/cab
    計程車

19. taxi stand
    計程車站
20. taxi driver
    計程車司機
21. meter
    車程計費表
22. taxi license
    計程車執照
23. ferry
    渡船

More vocabulary

hail a taxi: to get a taxi driver's attention by raising your hand

miss the bus: to arrive at the bus stop late

Talk about how you and your friends come to school.

I take _the bus_ to school.　　He _drives_ to school.

You take _the train_.　　　　She _walks_ to school.

We take _the subway_.　　　They _ride_ bikes.

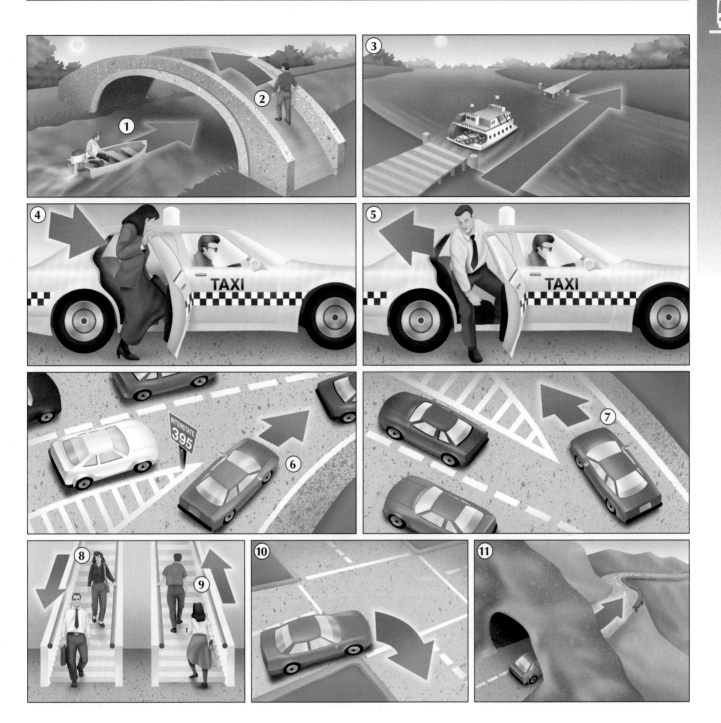

1. **under** the bridge
在橋下

2. **over** the bridge
在橋上

3. **across** the water
涉水

4. **into** the taxi
坐進計程汽車

5. **out of** the taxi
從計程車內**出來**

6. **onto** the highway
上公路

7. **off** the highway
下公路

8. **down** the stairs
下樓

9. **up** the stairs
上樓

10. **around** the corner
在角落**邊**

11. **through** the tunnel
通過隧道

Grammar point: *into, out of, on, off*

We say, *get **into** a taxi or a car.*
But we say, *get **on** a bus, a train, or a plane.*

We say, *get **out of** a taxi or a car.*
But we say, *get **off** a bus, a train, or a plane.*

1. **subcompact**
   迷你型汽車

2. **compact**
   小型汽車

3. **midsize car**
   中型汽車

4. **full-size car**
   大型汽車

5. **convertible**
   敞篷汽車

MPV   multi purpose vehicle

6. **sports car**
   跑車

7. **pickup truck**
   小卡車

8. **station wagon**
   旅行車

9. **SUV (sports utility vehicle)**
   越野多功能汽車   休旅車

10. **minivan**   MPV
    小型廂型車

11. **camper**
    野營用汽車

12. **dump truck**
    垃圾車

13. **tow truck**
    拖吊車

14. **moving van**
    搬家貨車

15. **tractor trailer/semi**
    牽引機拖車／半型

16. **cab**
    計程車

17. **trailer**
    拖車

station wagon   旅行車.

More vocabulary

make: the name of the company that makes the car

model: the style of car

Share your answers.

1. What is your favorite kind of car?

2. What kind of car is good for a big family? for a single person?

Directions　方向

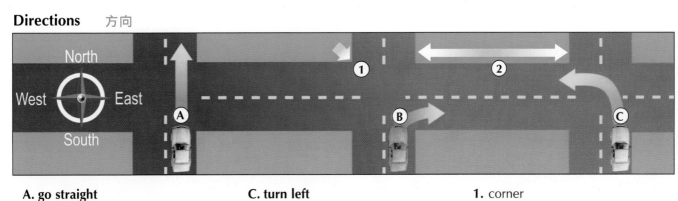

North
West　East
South

A. go straight
直走

B. turn right
右轉

C. turn left
左轉

1. corner
街角

2. block
街區

Signs　號誌

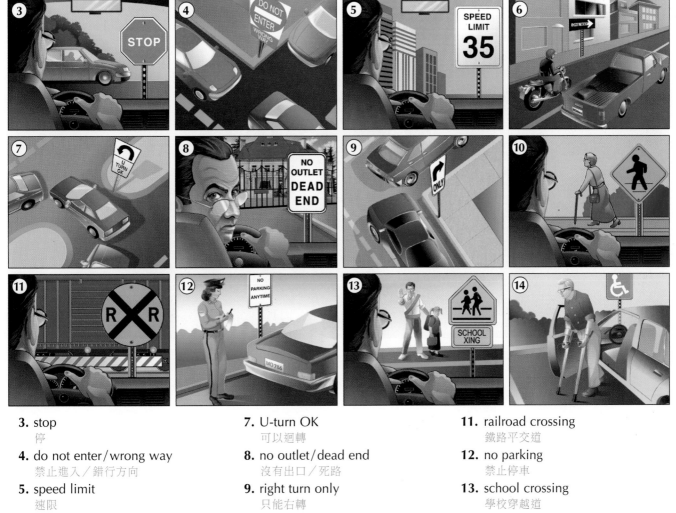

3. stop
停

4. do not enter / wrong way
禁止進入／錯行方向

5. speed limit
速限

6. one way
單行道

7. U-turn OK
可以迴轉

8. no outlet / dead end
沒有出口／死路

9. right turn only
只能右轉

10. pedestrian crossing
行人穿越道

11. railroad crossing
鐵路平交道

12. no parking
禁止停車

13. school crossing
學校穿越道

14. handicapped parking
殘障人士專用停車

More vocabulary

right-of-way: the right to go first

yield: to give another person or car the right-of-way

Share your answers.

1. Which traffic signs are the same in your country?

2. Do pedestrians have the right-of-way in your city?

3. What is the speed limit in front of your school? your home?

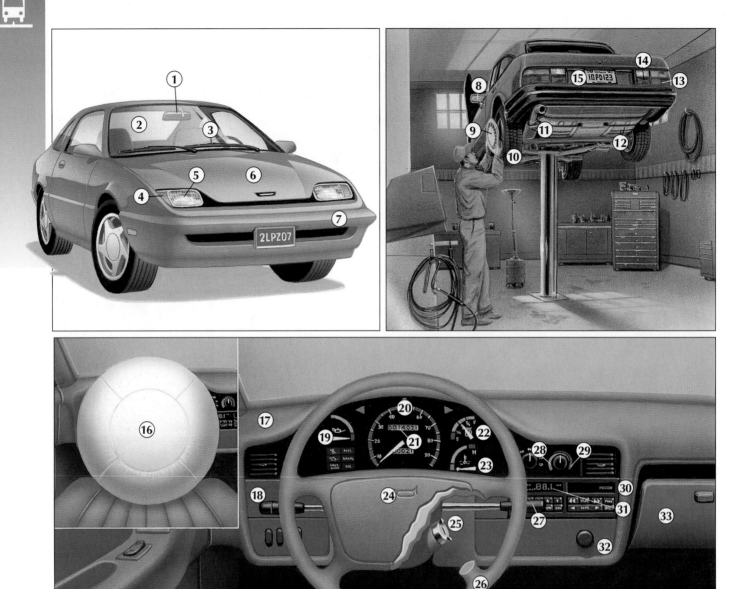

1. rearview mirror 後視鏡	**10.** tire 輪胎	**19.** oil gauge 機油計量表	**28.** air conditioning 冷氣
2. windshield 擋風玻璃	**11.** muffler 消音器	**20.** speedometer 速率表	**29.** heater 暖氣
3. windshield wipers 擋風玻璃雨刷	**12.** gas tank 油箱	**21.** odometer 里程表	**30.** tape deck 錄音帶卡匣
4. turn signal 轉向指示燈	**13.** brake light 煞車燈	**22.** gas gauge 汽油／油料計量表	**31.** radio 收音機
5. headlight 車前燈	**14.** taillight 車尾燈	**23.** temperature gauge 溫度表	**32.** cigarette lighter 香煙點火器
6. hood 引擎蓋	**15.** license plate 汽車牌照	**24.** horn 喇叭	**33.** glove compartment 工具箱
7. bumper 保險桿	**16.** air bag 安全氣囊	**25.** ignition 點火電門	
8. sideview mirror 側翼後視鏡	**17.** dashboard 儀表板	**26.** steering wheel 方向盤	
9. hubcap 車輪蓋	**18.** turn signal 轉向指示燈	**27.** gearshift 變速桿	

34. lock
鎖

35. front seat
前座

36. seat belt
安全帶

37. shoulder harness
肩帶

38. backseat
後座

39. child safety seat
孩童安全座椅

40. fuel injection system
燃料噴射系統

41. engine
引擎

42. radiator
冷卻器

43. battery
電瓶

44. emergency brake
緊急煞車

45. clutch*
離合器

46. brake pedal
煞車踏板

47. accelerator/gas pedal
油門踏板

48. stick shift
手排檔

49. trunk
後車箱

50. lug wrench
拉扳鉗

51. jack
千斤頂

52. jumper cables
升壓電纜

53. spare tire
備用輪胎

54. The car needs **gas**.
車子需要**汽油**。

55. The car needs **oil**.
車子需要**機油**。

56. The radiator needs **coolant**.
冷卻器需要加裝**冷卻劑**。

57. The car needs **a smog check**.
車子需要**排氣檢查**。

58. The battery needs **recharging**.
電瓶需要**充電**。

59. The tires need **air**.
輪胎需要**打氣**。

*Note: Standard transmission cars have a clutch; automatic transmission cars do not.

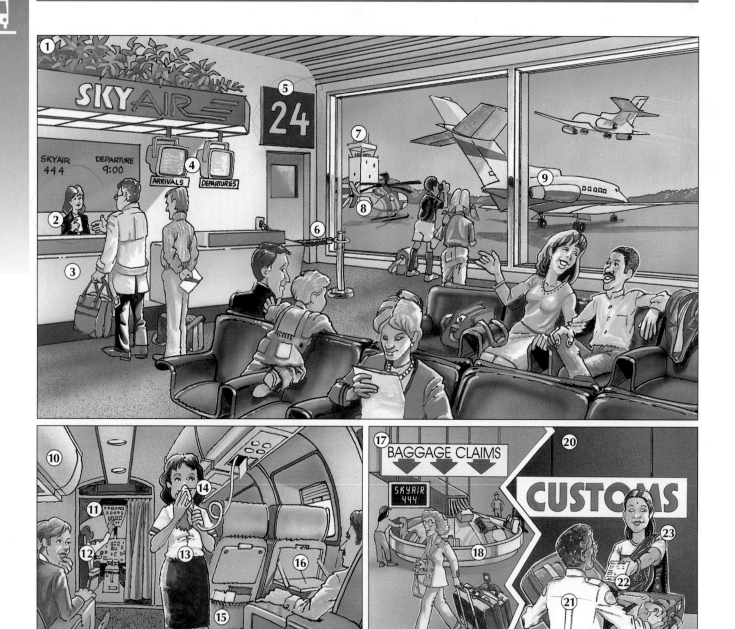

1. airline terminal
   航空公司站

2. airline representative
   航空公司地勤人員

3. check-in counter
   登記櫃台

4. arrival and departure monitors
   抵達及起飛螢幕

5. gate
   登機門

6. boarding area
   登機區

7. control tower
   控制塔台

8. helicopter
   直升機

9. airplane
   飛機

10. overhead compartment
    上方行李箱

11. cockpit
    駕駛艙

12. pilot
    飛行員

13. flight attendant
    空服員

14. oxygen mask
    氧氣面罩

15. airsickness bag
    暈機嘔吐袋

16. tray table
    餐桌

17. baggage claim area
    行李領取處

18. carousel
    轉盤

19. luggage carrier
    行李運送員

20. customs
    海關

21. customs officer
    海關人員

22. declaration form
    報關表

23. passenger
    乘客

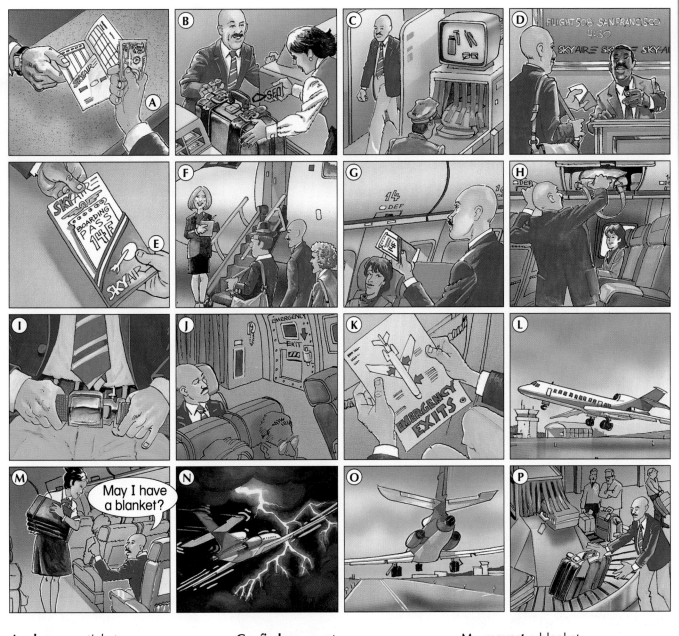

A. **buy** your ticket
訂購機票

B. **check** your bags
檢查行李

C. **go through** security
通過安全檢查

D. **check in** at the gate
登機門前報到

E. **get** your boarding pass
領取登機證

F. **board** the plane
上飛機

G. **find** your seat
找座位

H. **stow** your carry-on bag
放好手提行李

I. **fasten** your seat belt
繫上安全帶

J. **look for** the emergency exit
尋找緊急出口

K. **look at** the emergency card
閱讀緊急情況說明卡

L. **take off / leave**
起飛

M. **request** a blanket
要求毯子

N. **experience** turbulence
遇到氣流　3 jwd

O. **land / arrive**
降落／抵達

P. **claim** your baggage
領取行李

buckle head 皮帶頭

what sort of things go "beep" when you walk
throug the scanner?

More vocabulary

destination: the place the passenger is going
departure time: the time the plane takes off
arrival time: the time the plane lands

direct flight: a plane trip between two cities with no stops
轉飛機 **stopover:** a stop before reaching the destination,
sometimes to change planes

111

1. public school
公立學校

2. private school
私立學校

3. parochial school
教會學校

4. preschool
托兒所

5. elementary school
小學

6. middle school/
junior high school
中學／初中

7. high school
高中

8. adult school
成人學校

9. vocational school/trade school
職業學校

10. college/university
專科學校／大學

Note: In the U.S. most children begin school at age 5 (in kindergarten) and graduate from high school at 17 or 18.

More vocabulary

When students graduate from a college or university they receive a **degree**:

Bachelor's degree—usually 4 years of study

Master's degree—an additional 1–3 years of study

Doctorate—an additional 3–5 years of study

community college: a two-year college where students can get an Associate of Arts degree

graduate school: a school in a university where students study for their master's and doctorates

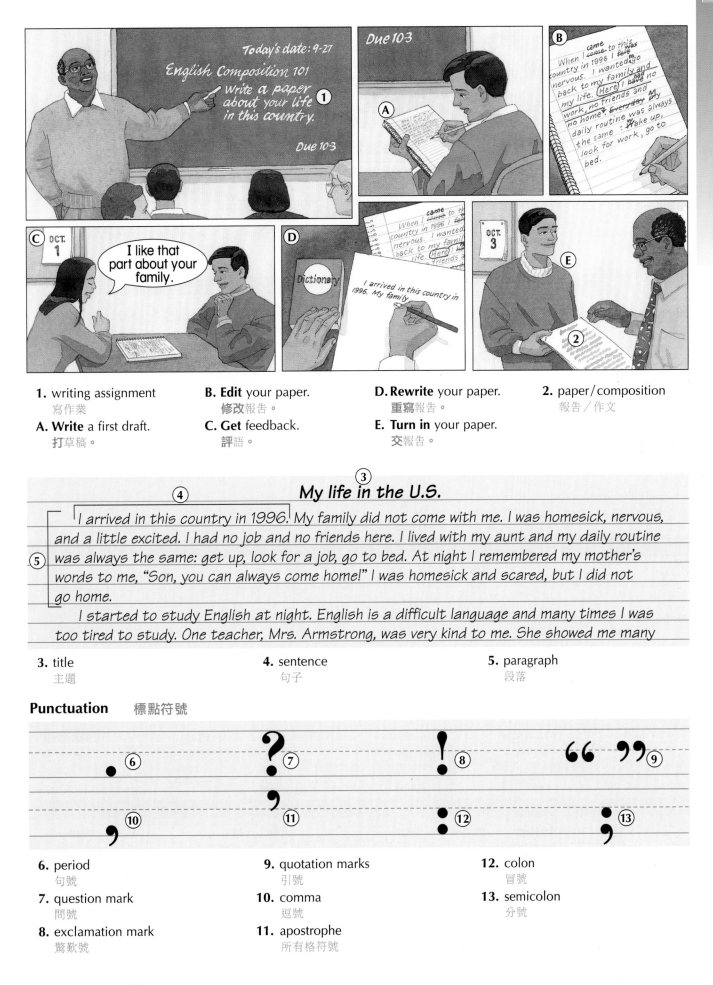

1. writing assignment
寫作業

A. **Write** a first draft.
打草稿。

B. **Edit** your paper.
修改報告。

C. **Get** feedback.
評語。

D. **Rewrite** your paper.
重寫報告。

E. **Turn in** your paper.
交報告。

2. paper/composition
報告／作文

My life in the U.S.

I arrived in this country in 1996. My family did not come with me. I was homesick, nervous, and a little excited. I had no job and no friends here. I lived with my aunt and my daily routine was always the same: get up, look for a job, go to bed. At night I remembered my mother's words to me, "Son, you can always come home!" I was homesick and scared, but I did not go home.

I started to study English at night. English is a difficult language and many times I was too tired to study. One teacher, Mrs. Armstrong, was very kind to me. She showed me many

3. title
主題

4. sentence
句子

5. paragraph
段落

Punctuation　標點符號

6. period
句號

7. question mark
問號

8. exclamation mark
驚歎號

9. quotation marks
引號

10. comma
逗號

11. apostrophe
所有格符號

12. colon
冒號

13. semicolon
分號

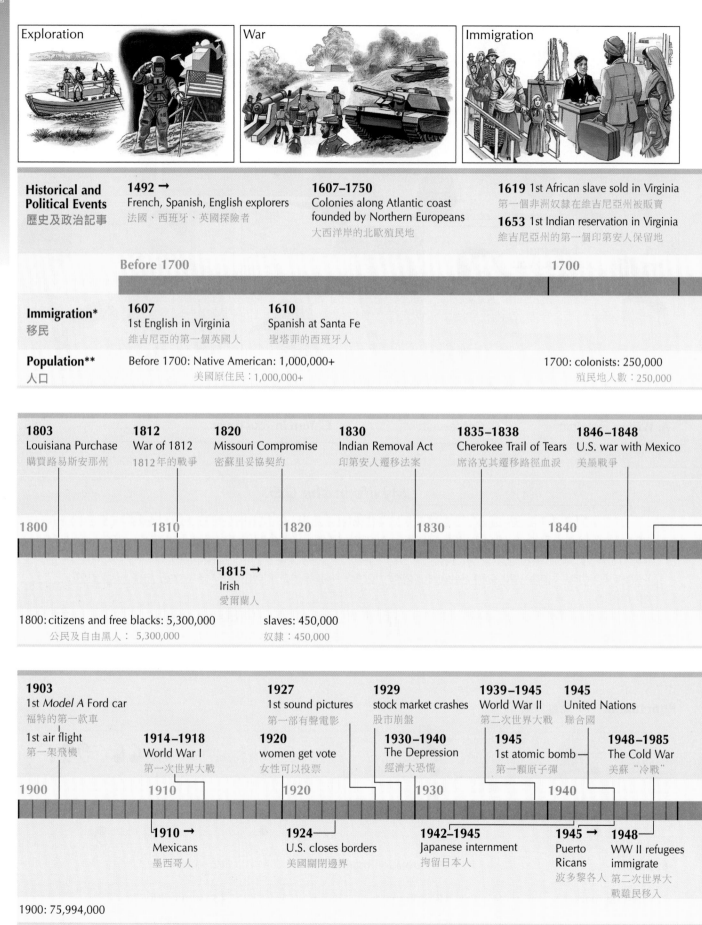

Exploration

War

Immigration

| Historical and Political Events 歷史及政治記事 | **1492 →** French, Spanish, English explorers 法國、西班牙、英國探險者 | **1607–1750** Colonies along Atlantic coast founded by Northern Europeans 大西洋岸的北歐殖民地 | **1619** 1st African slave sold in Virginia 第一個非洲奴隸在維吉尼亞州被販賣 **1653** 1st Indian reservation in Virginia 維吉尼亞州的第一個印第安人保留地 |

Before 1700　　　　　　　　　　　　　　　　　　　　**1700**

| Immigration* 移民 | **1607** 1st English in Virginia 維吉尼亞的第一個英國人 | **1610** Spanish at Santa Fe 聖塔菲的西班牙人 | |

| Population** 人口 | Before 1700: Native American: 1,000,000+ 美國原住民：1,000,000+ | | 1700: colonists: 250,000 殖民地人數：250,000 |

| **1803** Louisiana Purchase 購買路易斯安那州 | **1812** War of 1812 1812年的戰爭 | **1820** Missouri Compromise 密蘇里妥協契約 | **1830** Indian Removal Act 印第安人遷移法案 | **1835–1838** Cherokee Trail of Tears 席洛克其遷移路徑血淚 | **1846–1848** U.S. war with Mexico 美墨戰爭 |

1800　　　　1810　　　　1820　　　　1830　　　　1840

1815 → Irish 愛爾蘭人

1800: citizens and free blacks: 5,300,000　　slaves: 450,000
公民及自由黑人：5,300,000　　奴隸：450,000

| **1903** 1st *Model A* Ford car 福特的第一款車 1st air flight 第一架飛機 | **1927** 1st sound pictures 第一部有聲電影 | **1929** stock market crashes 股市崩盤 | **1939–1945** World War II 第二次世界大戰 | **1945** United Nations 聯合國 |

| **1914–1918** World War I 第一次世界大戰 | **1920** women get vote 女性可以投票 | **1930–1940** The Depression 經濟大恐慌 | **1945** 1st atomic bomb 第一顆原子彈 | **1948–1985** The Cold War 美蘇 "冷戰" |

1900　　　　1910　　　　1920　　　　1930　　　　1940

1910 → Mexicans 墨西哥人

1924 U.S. closes borders 美國關閉邊界

1942–1945 Japanese internment 拘留日本人

1945 → Puerto Ricans 波多黎各人

1948 WW II refugees immigrate 第二次世界大戰難民移入

1900: 75,994,000

*Immigration dates indicate a time when large numbers of that group first began to immigrate to the U.S.
**All population figures before 1790 are estimates. Figures after 1790 are based on the official U.S. census.

Movement

Election

Invention

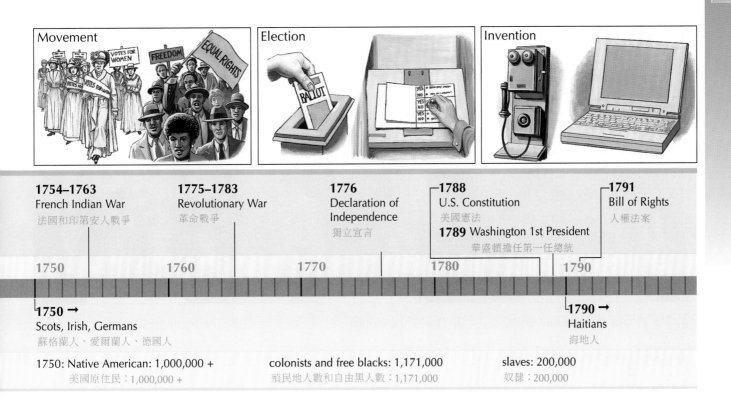

1754–1763
French Indian War
法國和印第安人戰爭

1775–1783
Revolutionary War
革命戰爭

1776
Declaration of Independence
獨立宣言

1788
U.S. Constitution
美國憲法

1789 Washington 1st President
華盛頓擔任第一任總統

1791
Bill of Rights
人權法案

1750   1760   1770   1780   1790

1750 →
Scots, Irish, Germans
蘇格蘭人、愛爾蘭人、德國人

1790 →
Haitians
海地人

1750: Native American: 1,000,000 +
美國原住民：1,000,000 +

colonists and free blacks: 1,171,000
殖民地人數和自由黑人數：1,171,000

slaves: 200,000
奴隸：200,000

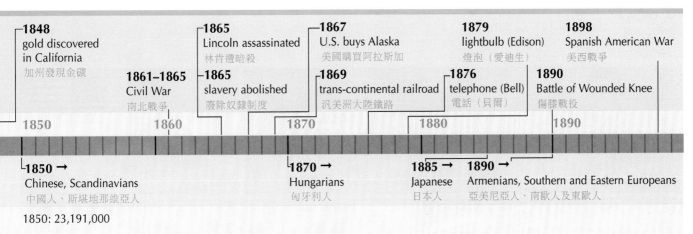

1848
gold discovered in California
加州發現金礦

1865
Lincoln assassinated
林肯遭暗殺

1867
U.S. buys Alaska
美國購買阿拉斯加

1879
lightbulb (Edison)
燈泡（愛迪生）

1898
Spanish American War
美西戰爭

1861–1865
Civil War
南北戰爭

1865
slavery abolished
廢除奴隸制度

1869
trans-continental railroad
汎美洲大陸鐵路

1876
telephone (Bell)
電話（貝爾）

1890
Battle of Wounded Knee
傷膝戰役

1850   1860   1870   1880   1890

1850 →
Chinese, Scandinavians
中國人、斯堪地那維亞人

1870 →
Hungarians
匈牙利人

1885 →
Japanese
日本人

1890 →
Armenians, Southern and Eastern Europeans
亞美尼亞人、南歐人及東歐人

1850: 23,191,000

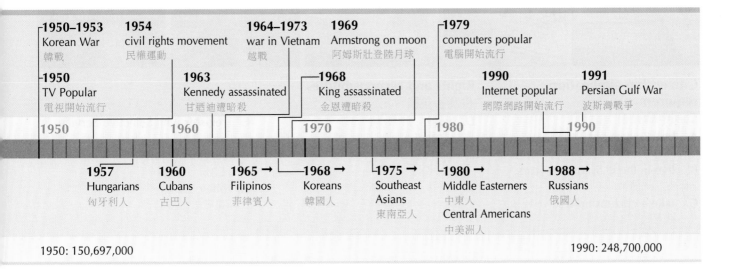

1950–1953
Korean War
韓戰

1954
civil rights movement
民權運動

1964–1973
war in Vietnam
越戰

1969
Armstrong on moon
阿姆斯壯登陸月球

1979
computers popular
電腦開始流行

1950
TV Popular
電視開始流行

1963
Kennedy assassinated
甘迺迪遭暗殺

1968
King assassinated
金恩遭暗殺

1990
Internet popular
網際網路開始流行

1991
Persian Gulf War
波斯灣戰爭

1950   1960   1970   1980   1990

1957
Hungarians
匈牙利人

1960
Cubans
古巴人

1965 →
Filipinos
菲律賓人

1968 →
Koreans
韓國人

1975 →
Southeast Asians
東南亞人

1980 →
Middle Easterners
中東人
Central Americans
中美洲人

1988 →
Russians
俄國人

1950: 150,697,000

1990: 248,700,000

BRANCHES OF GOVERNMENT

Legislative | Executive | Judicial

1. The House of Representatives
眾議院

2. congresswoman / congressman
國會女議員／國會議員

3. The Senate
參議院

4. senator
參議員

5. The White House
白宮

6. president
總統

7. vice president
副總統

8. The Supreme Court
最高法院

9. chief justice
大法官

10. justices
法官

Citizenship application requirements
公民申請資格

A. **be** 18 years old
年滿18歲

B. **live** in the U.S. for five years
在美國居留五年

C. **take** a citizenship test
參加公民考試

Rights and responsibilities
權利和義務

D. **vote**
投票

E. **pay** taxes
納稅

F. **register** with Selective Service*
役男登記

G. **serve** on a jury
擔任陪審團員

H. **obey** the law
遵守法律

*Note: All males 18 to 26 who live in the U.S. are required to register with Selective Service.

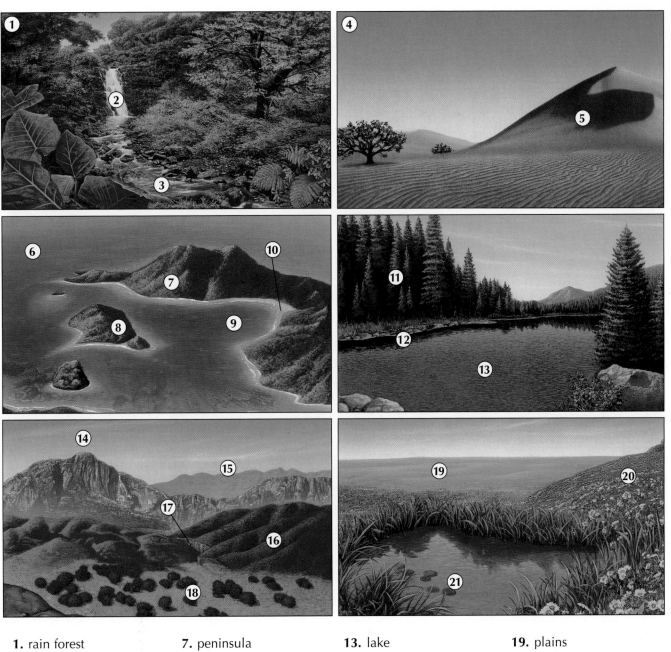

1. rain forest
雨林

2. waterfall
瀑布

3. river
河流

4. desert
沙漠

5. sand dune
沙丘

6. ocean
海洋

7. peninsula
半島

8. island
島嶼

9. bay
海灣

10. beach
沙灘

11. forest
森林

12. shore
湖邊／海邊

13. lake
湖泊

14. mountain peak
山頂

15. mountain range
山脈

16. hills
山坡

17. canyon
峽谷

18. valley
山谷

19. plains
平原

20. meadow
草原

21. pond
池塘

More vocabulary

a body of water: a river, lake, or ocean

stream/creek: a very small river

Talk about where you live and where you like to go.

I live in a valley. There is a lake nearby.

I like to go to the beach.

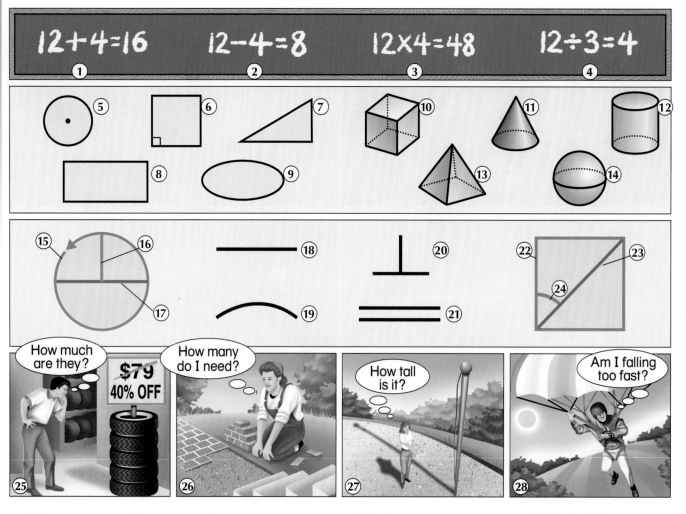

Operations
演算

1. addition
加法

2. subtraction
減法

3. multiplication
乘法

4. division
除法

Shapes
形狀

5. circle
圓形

6. square
正方形

7. triangle
三角形

8. rectangle
長方形

9. oval/ellipse
橢圓形

Solids
立體

10. cube
正方體

11. cone
圓錐體

12. cylinder
圓柱體

13. pyramid
角錐體

14. sphere
球體

Parts of a circle
圓形各部名稱

15. circumference
圓周

16. radius
半徑

17. diameter
直徑

Lines
線

18. straight
直線

19. curved
曲線

20. perpendicular
垂直線

21. parallel
平行線

Parts of a square
正方形各部名稱

22. side
邊

23. diagonal
對角線

24. angle
角

Types of math
數學種類

25. algebra
代數

26. geometry
幾何學

27. trigonometry
三角學

28. calculus
微積分

More vocabulary

total: the answer to an addition problem

difference: the answer to a subtraction problem

product: the answer to a multiplication problem

quotient: the answer to a division problem

pi (π): the number when you divide the circumference of a circle by its diameter (approximately = 3.14)

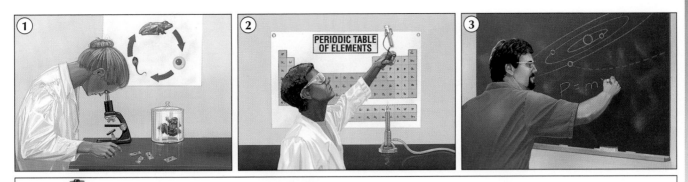

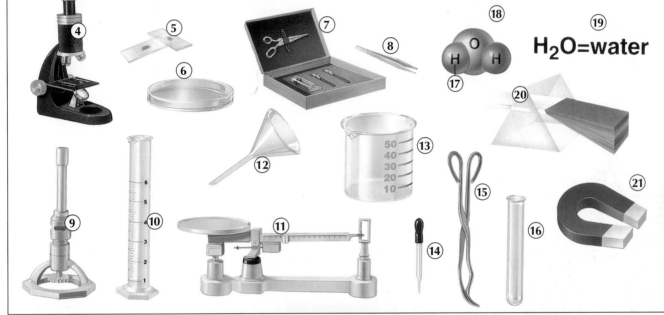

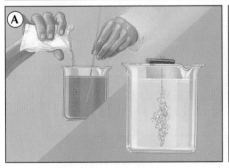

1. biology
   生物

2. chemistry
   化學

3. physics
   物理

4. microscope
   顯微鏡

5. slide
   載物玻璃片

6. petri dish
   培養皿

7. dissection kit
   解剖器具組盒

8. forceps
   鉗子

9. Bunsen burner
   本生燈

10. graduated cylinder
    刻度筒

11. balance
    天平

12. funnel
    漏斗

13. beaker
    燒杯

14. dropper
    滴管

15. crucible tongs
    坩堝夾

16. test tube
    試管

17. atom
    原子

18. molecule
    分子

19. formula
    公式

20. prism
    稜鏡

21. magnet
    磁鐵

A. **do** an experiment
   作實驗

B. **observe**
   觀察

C. **record** results
   記錄結果

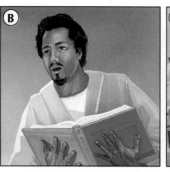

A. play an instrument
演奏樂器

B. sing a song
唱歌

1. orchestra
管絃樂團

2. rock band
搖滾樂團

Woodwinds

Strings

Brass

Percussion

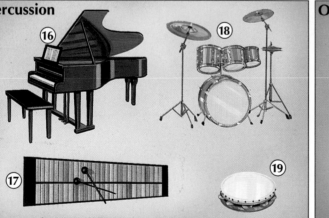

Other Instruments

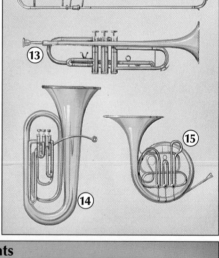

3. flute 笛子	**8.** violin 小提琴	**13.** trumpet/horn 喇叭	**18.** drums 鼓
4. clarinet 單簧管	**9.** cello 大提琴	**14.** tuba 低音大喇叭	**19.** tambourine 鈴鼓
5. oboe 雙簧管	**10.** bass 低音提琴	**15.** French horn 法國號	**20.** electric keyboard 電子琴
6. bassoon 巴松管	**11.** guitar 吉他	**16.** piano 鋼琴	**21.** accordion 手風琴
7. saxophone 薩克斯風	**12.** trombone 伸縮喇叭	**17.** xylophone 木琴	**22.** organ 風琴

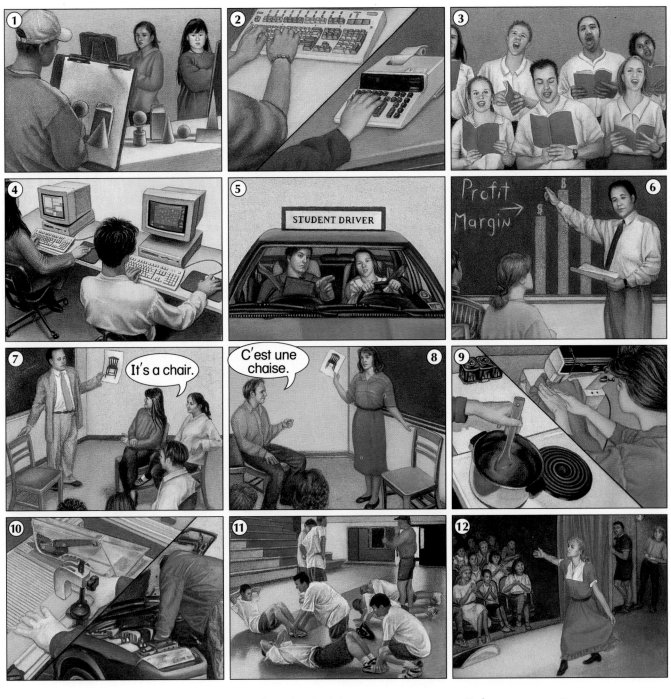

1. art
   藝術

2. business education
   商業教育

3. chorus
   合唱團

4. computer science
   電腦科學

5. driver's education
   駕駛教育

6. economics
   經濟學

7. English as a second language
   英語作為第二外語

8. foreign language
   外語

9. home economics
   家政

10. industrial arts/shop
    工藝／作坊

11. PE (physical education)
    體育

12. theater arts
    戲劇藝術

More vocabulary

core course: a subject students have to take

elective: a subject students choose to take

Share your answers.

1. What are your favorite subjects?

2. In your opinion, what subjects are most important? Why?

3. What foreign languages are taught in your school?

ATLANTIC OCEAN

BERMUDA

cap cod 鱈角

GREENLAND

Labrador Sea

Baffin Bay

ARCTIC OCEAN

Beaufort Sea

Queen Elizabeth Islands

Northwest Territories

Yukon Territory

Alaska (US)

Gulf of Alaska

Hudson Bay

Newfoundland

Gulf of St. Lawrence

Prince Edward Island

Nova Scotia

New Brunswick

Maine

Vermont

New Hampshire

Massachusetts

Rhode Island

Connecticut

New York

New Jersey

Delaware

Maryland

WASHINGTON, D.C.

Pennsylvania

West Virginia

Virginia

North Carolina

South Carolina

Georgia

Ohio

Kentucky

Tennessee

Arkansas

Québec

Ontario

OTTAWA

Michigan

Michigan

Wisconsin

Illinois

Indiana

Missouri

Minnesota

Iowa

Manitoba

Saskatchewan

Alberta

British Columbia

CANADA

North Dakota

South Dakota

Nebraska

Kansas

Oklahoma

UNITED STATES OF AMERICA

Montana

Wyoming

Colorado

New Mexico

Idaho

Utah

Arizona

Washington

Oregon

Nevada

California

Hawaii (US)

① ② ③ ④ ⑤ ⑥ ⑦ ⑧ ⑨ ⑩ ⑪

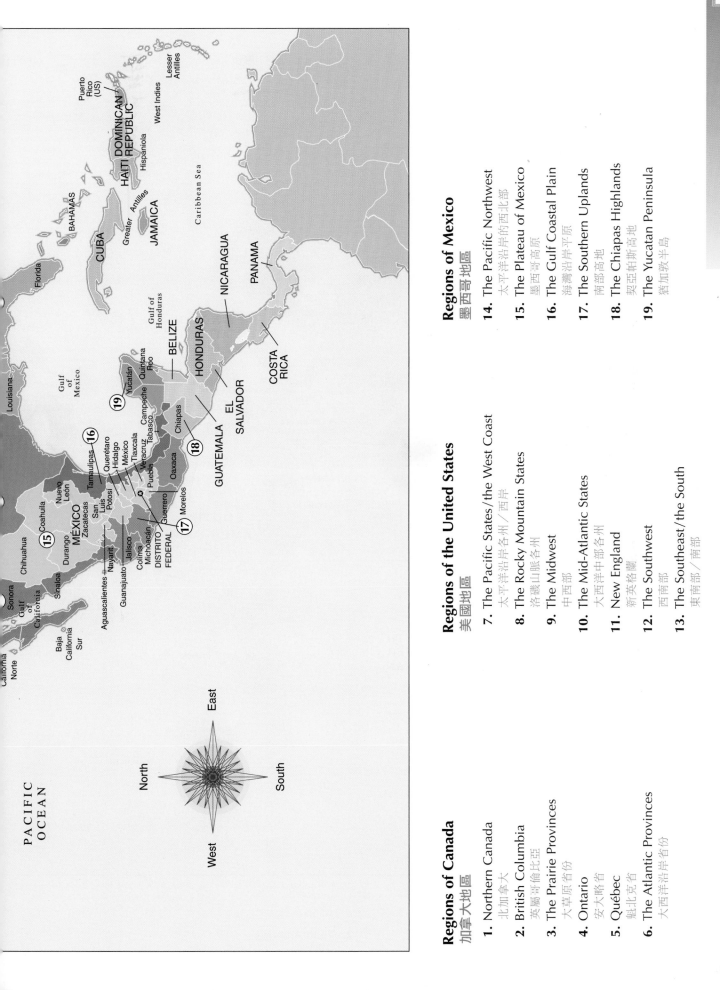

PACIFIC OCEAN

North
West
South
East

California Norte

Baja California Sur

Sonora

Gulf of California

Chihuahua

Sinaloa

Durango

⑮

Coahuila

Nuevo León

Zacatecas

MÉXICO

San Luis Potosí

Aguascalientes

Nayarit

Jalisco

Colima

Guanajuato

Michoacán

DISTRITO FEDERAL

⑰

Morelos

Guerrero

Querétaro

Hidalgo

México

Puebla

Tlaxcala

Veracruz

Oaxaca

⑱

Chiapas

Tabasco

Campeche

⑯

Tamaulipas

⑲

Yucatán

Quintana Roo

Louisiana

Gulf of Mexico

Florida

BAHAMAS

CUBA

Greater Antilles

JAMAICA

HAITI

DOMINICAN REPUBLIC

Hispaniola

West Indies

Puerto Rico (US)

Lesser Antilles

Caribbean Sea

Gulf of Honduras

BELIZE

GUATEMALA

EL SALVADOR

HONDURAS

NICARAGUA

COSTA RICA

PANAMA

Regions of Canada
加拿大地區

1. Northern Canada
   北加拿大

2. British Columbia
   英屬哥倫比亞

3. The Prairie Provinces
   大草原省份

4. Ontario
   安大略省

5. Québec
   魁北克省

6. The Atlantic Provinces
   大西洋沿岸省份

Regions of the United States
美國地區

7. The Pacific States / the West Coast
   太平洋沿岸各州 / 西岸

8. The Rocky Mountain States
   洛磯山脈各州

9. The Midwest
   中西部

10. The Mid-Atlantic States
    大西洋中部各州

11. New England
    新英格蘭

12. The Southwest
    西南部

13. The Southeast / the South
    東南部 / 南部

Regions of Mexico
墨西哥地區

14. The Pacific Northwest
    太平洋沿岸的西北部

15. The Plateau of Mexico
    墨西哥高原

16. The Gulf Coastal Plain
    海灣沿岸平原

17. The Southern Uplands
    南部高地

18. The Chiapas Highlands
    契亞帕斯高地

19. The Yucatan Peninsula
    猶加敦半島

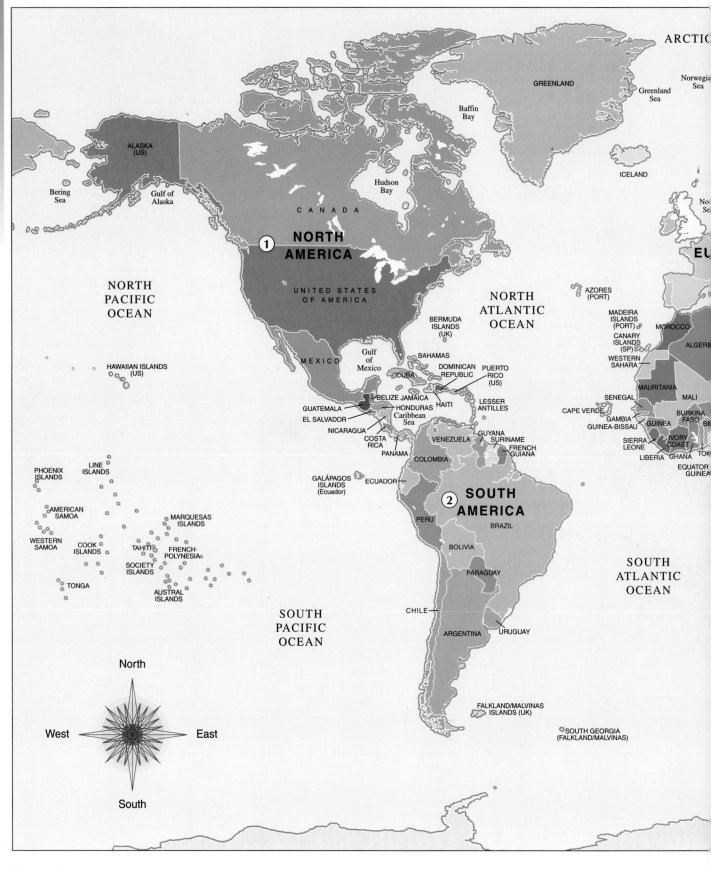

Continents
大陸

1. North America
北美洲

2. South America
南美洲

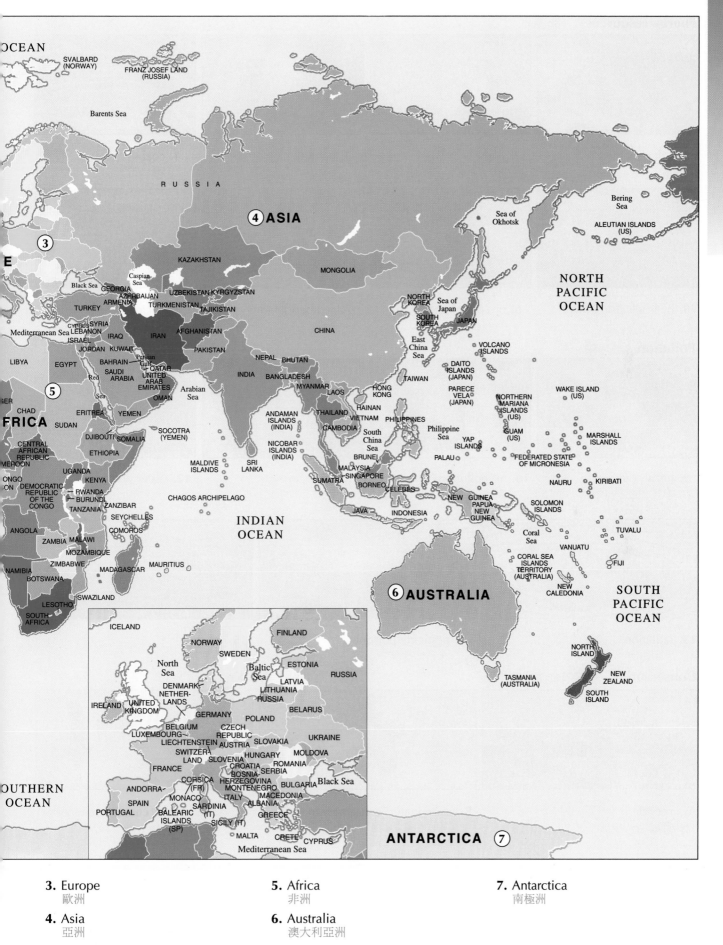

OCEAN

SVALBARD
(NORWAY)

FRANZ JOSEF LAND
(RUSSIA)

Barents Sea

R U S S I A

④ ASIA

③

E

KAZAKHSTAN

MONGOLIA

Bering
Sea

Sea of
Okhotsk

ALEUTIAN ISLANDS
(US)

NORTH
PACIFIC
OCEAN

Black Sea GEORGIA
AZERBAIJAN
ARMENIA
TURKEY

Caspian
Sea

UZBEKISTAN KYRGYZSTAN
TURKMENISTAN
TAJIKISTAN

NORTH
KOREA
SOUTH
KOREA

Sea of
Japan

JAPAN

Mediterranean Sea
CYPRUS
LEBANON
ISRAEL
JORDAN
SYRIA
IRAQ
KUWAIT

IRAN
AFGHANISTAN

CHINA

East
China
Sea

TAIWAN

VOLCANO
ISLANDS

DAITO
ISLANDS
(JAPAN)

PARECE
VELA
(JAPAN)

WAKE ISLAND
(US)

LIBYA

EGYPT

BAHRAIN
QATAR
SAUDI
ARABIA
UNITED
ARAB
EMIRATES

Persian
Gulf

PAKISTAN

NEPAL BHUTAN

BANGLADESH

INDIA

MYANMAR

LAOS

HONG
KONG

HAINAN

VIETNAM

South
China
Sea

PHILIPPINES

Philippine
Sea

YAP
ISLANDS

NORTHERN
MARIANA
ISLANDS
(US)

GUAM
(US)

MARSHALL
ISLANDS

⑤

Red
Sea

OMAN

Arabian
Sea

THAILAND

CAMBODIA

PALAU

FEDERATED STATE
OF MICRONESIA

FRICA

CHAD

SUDAN

ERITREA

YEMEN

DJIBOUTI SOMALIA

SOCOTRA
(YEMEN)

ANDAMAN
ISLANDS
(INDIA)

NICOBAR
ISLANDS
(INDIA)

BRUNEI

NAURU

KIRIBATI

CENTRAL
AFRICAN
REPUBLIC

CAMEROON

ETHIOPIA

MALDIVE
ISLANDS

SRI
LANKA

MALAYSIA
SINGAPORE
BORNEO

CELEBES

NEW GUINEA
PAPUA
NEW
GUINEA

SOLOMON
ISLANDS

CONGO
ON

UGANDA
KENYA

DEMOCRATIC
REPUBLIC
OF THE
CONGO

RWANDA
BURUNDI

ZANZIBAR

TANZANIA

SEYCHELLES

CHAGOS ARCHIPELAGO

SUMATRA

JAVA

INDONESIA

TUVALU

VANUATU

FIJI

ANGOLA

ZAMBIA MALAWI

COMOROS

INDIAN
OCEAN

Coral
Sea

CORAL SEA
ISLANDS
TERRITORY
(AUSTRALIA)

NEW
CALEDONIA

SOUTH
PACIFIC
OCEAN

MOZAMBIQUE

ZIMBABWE

MAURITIUS

NAMIBIA
BOTSWANA

MADAGASCAR

⑥ AUSTRALIA

LESOTHO
SWAZILAND

SOUTH
AFRICA

NORTH
ISLAND

TASMANIA
(AUSTRALIA)

NEW
ZEALAND

SOUTH
ISLAND

ICELAND

NORWAY

FINLAND

SWEDEN

North
Sea

Baltic
Sea

ESTONIA

RUSSIA

DENMARK
NETHER-
LANDS

LATVIA
LITHUANIA
RUSSIA

IRELAND
UNITED
KINGDOM

GERMANY

POLAND

BELARUS

SOUTHERN
OCEAN

BELGIUM
LUXEMBOURG
LIECHTENSTEIN
SWITZER-
LAND

CZECH
REPUBLIC
AUSTRIA
SLOVENIA
HUNGARY

SLOVAKIA

UKRAINE

MOLDOVA

ROMANIA

FRANCE

CROATIA

SERBIA

ANDORRA

SPAIN

CORSICA
(FR)
MONACO
SARDINIA
(IT)

BOSNIA
HERZEGOVINA
MONTENEGRO
ITALY

BULGARIA

Black Sea

MACEDONIA
ALBANIA

PORTUGAL

BALEARIC
ISLANDS
(SP)

SICILY (IT)

MALTA

GREECE

CRETE

CYPRUS

Mediterranean Sea

ANTARCTICA ⑦

3. Europe
歐洲

4. Asia
亞洲

5. Africa
非洲

6. Australia
澳大利亞洲

7. Antarctica
南極洲

Energy resources 能源

1. solar energy
太陽能

2. wind
風

3. natural gas
天然氣

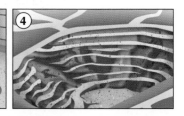

4. coal
煤

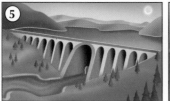

5. hydroelectric power
水力發電

6. oil/petroleum
石油

7. geothermal energy
地熱

8. nuclear energy
核電

Pollution 污染

9. hazardous waste
具危害性廢棄物

10. air pollution/smog
空氣污染／廢氣

11. acid rain
酸雨

12. water pollution
水污染

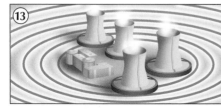

13. radiation
放射線

14. pesticide poisoning
殺蟲劑毒害

15. oil spill
石油外溢

Conservation 保存能源

A. recycle
回收

B. save water／**conserve** water
省水／節約用水

C. save energy／**conserve** energy
省／節約能源

Share your answers.

1. How do you heat your home?

2. Do you have a gas stove or an electric stove?

3. What are some ways you can save energy when it's cold?

4. Do you recycle? What products do you recycle?

5. Does your market have recycling bins?

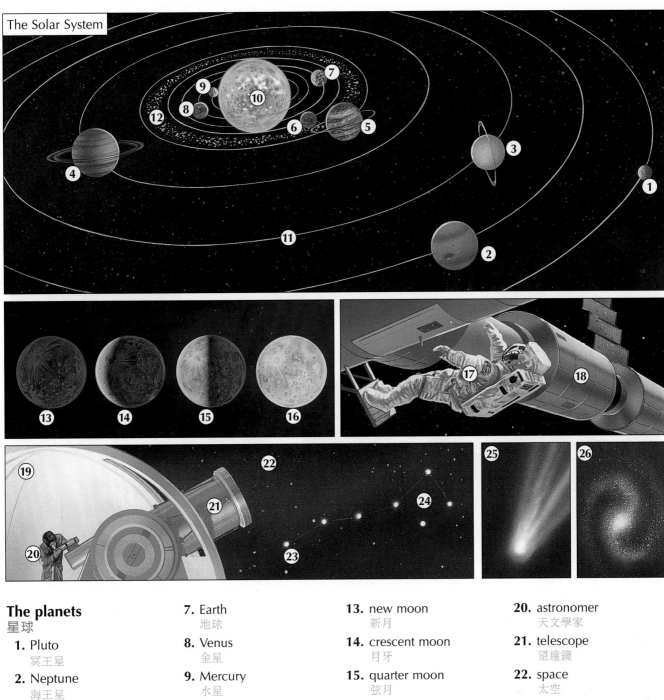

The Solar System

The planets
星球

1. Pluto
冥王星

2. Neptune
海王星

3. Uranus
天王星

4. Saturn
土星

5. Jupiter
木星

6. Mars
火星

7. Earth
地球

8. Venus
金星

9. Mercury
水星

10. sun
太陽

11. orbit
軌道

12. asteroid belt
行星帶

13. new moon
新月

14. crescent moon
月牙

15. quarter moon
弦月

16. full moon
滿月

17. astronaut
太空人

18. space station
太空站

19. observatory
天文台

20. astronomer
天文學家

21. telescope
望遠鏡

22. space
太空

23. star
星星

24. constellation
星座

25. comet
彗星

26. galaxy
銀河

More vocabulary

lunar eclipse: when the earth is between the sun and the moon

solar eclipse: when the moon is between the earth and the sun

Share your answers.

1. Do you know the names of any constellations?

2. How do you feel when you look up at the night sky?

3. Is the night sky in the U.S. the same as in your country?

Parts of a tree 樹木各部分名稱

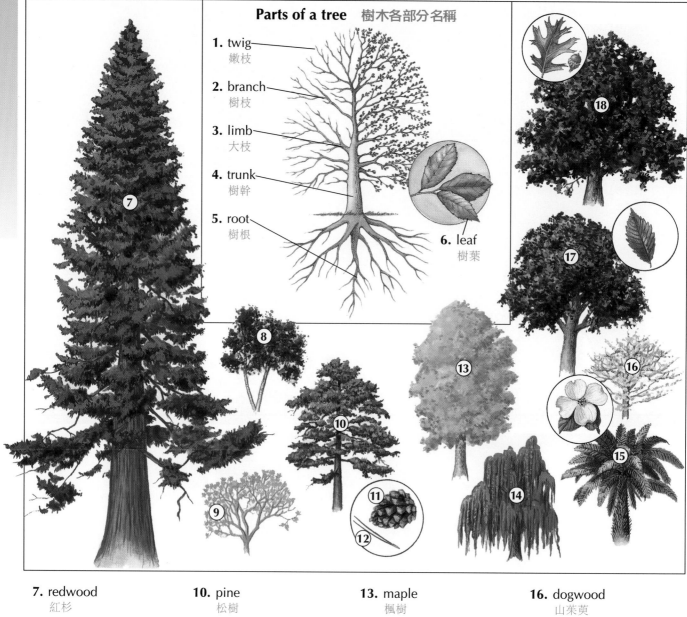

1. twig
嫩枝

2. branch
樹枝

3. limb
大枝

4. trunk
樹幹

5. root
樹根

6. leaf
樹葉

---

7. redwood
紅杉

8. birch
樺木

9. magnolia
木蘭

10. pine
松樹

11. pinecone
松果

12. needle
樹針

13. maple
楓樹

14. willow
柳樹

15. palm
棕櫚樹

16. dogwood
山茱萸

17. elm
榆木

18. oak
橡木

Plants 植物

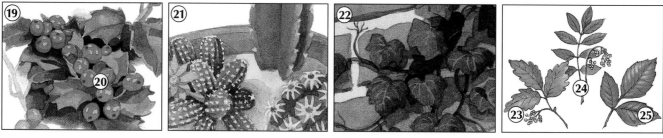

19. holly
冬青屬灌木

20. berries
漿果

21. cactus
仙人掌

22. vine
藤蔓

23. poison oak
野葛

24. poison sumac
美國毒漆

25. poison ivy
毒漆樹屬植物

Parts of a flower　花朵各部分名稱

1. seed 種子
2. seedling 播種
3. root 根
4. stem 莖
5. leaf 葉
6. bud 芽
7. flower 花朵
8. petal 花瓣
9. bulb 球莖

10. sunflower
向日葵

11. tulip
鬱金香

12. hibiscus
木槿

13. marigold
金盞草

14. daisy
雛菊

15. rose
玫瑰

16. gardenia
梔子

17. orchid
蘭花

18. carnation
康乃馨

19. chrysanthemum
菊花

20. iris
鳶尾

21. jasmine
茉莉花

22. violet
紫蘿蘭

23. poinsettia
聖誕紅

24. lily
百合花

25. crocus
番紅花

26. daffodil
水仙花

27. bouquet
花束

28. thorn
刺

29. houseplant
室內植物

Marine Life, Amphibians, and Reptiles 海洋生物、兩棲動物及爬蟲類

Parts of a fish 魚類各部

Sea animals 海洋動物

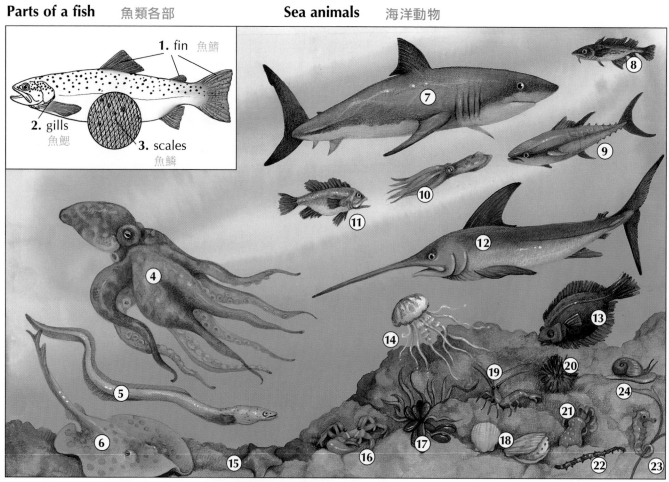

1. fin 魚鰭
2. gills 魚鰓
3. scales 魚鱗

4. octopus 章魚	**11.** bass 鱸魚	**18.** scallop 干貝
5. eel 鰻魚	**12.** swordfish 旗魚	**19.** shrimp 蝦
6. ray 魟魚	**13.** flounder 比目魚	**20.** sea urchin 海膽
7. shark 鯊魚	**14.** jellyfish 水母	**21.** sea anemone 海葵
8. cod 鱈魚	**15.** starfish 海星	**22.** worm 蟲
9. tuna 鮪魚	**16.** crab 螃蟹	**23.** sea horse 海馬
10. squid 魷魚	**17.** mussel 貽貝	**24.** snail 蝸牛

Amphibians 兩棲動物

25. frog 青蛙	**26.** newt 蠑螈	**27.** salamander 蠑螈	**28.** toad 蟾蜍

Sea mammals　海洋哺乳動物

29. whale
鯨魚

30. dolphin
海豚

31. porpoise
海豚

32. walrus
海象

33. seal
海豹

34. sea lion
海獅

35. otter
水獺

Reptiles　爬蟲類

36. alligator
短吻鱷

37. crocodile
鱷魚

38. rattlesnake
響尾蛇

39. garter snake
束帶蛇

40. cobra
眼鏡蛇

41. lizard
蜥蜴

42. turtle
烏龜

Parts of a bird 禽類各部名稱

1. beak/bill
   鳥嘴
2. wing
   翅膀
3. nest
   巢
4. claw
   爪
5. feather
   羽毛

6. owl 貓頭鷹	9. woodpecker 啄木鳥	12. penguin 企鵝	15. peacock 孔雀
7. blue jay 藍鴉	10. eagle 老鷹	13. duck 鴨	16. pigeon 鴿子
8. sparrow 麻雀	11. hummingbird 蜂鳥	14. goose 鵝	17. robin 知更鳥

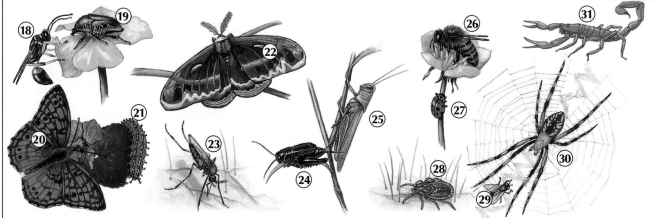

18. wasp 黃蜂	22. moth 蛾	26. honeybee 蜜蜂	30. spider 蜘蛛
19. beetle 甲蟲	23. mosquito 蚊子	27. ladybug 瓢蟲	31. scorpion 蠍
20. butterfly 蝴蝶	24. cricket 蟋蟀	28. tick 扁蝨	
21. caterpillar 毛蟲	25. grasshopper 蚱蜢	29. fly 蒼蠅	

Farm animals 農場動物

1. goat
山羊
2. donkey
驢子
3. cow
牛
4. horse
馬
5. hen
母雞
6. rooster
公雞
7. sheep
綿羊
8. pig
豬

Pets 寵物

9. cat
貓
10. kitten
小貓
11. dog
狗
12. puppy
小狗
13. rabbit
兔子
14. guinea pig
天竺鼠
15. parakeet
長尾小鸚鵡
16. goldfish
金魚

Rodents 齧齒類

17. mouse
老鼠
18. rat
大老鼠
19. gopher
地鼠
20. chipmunk
金花鼠
21. squirrel
松鼠
22. prairie dog
土撥鼠

More vocabulary

Wild animals live, eat, and raise their young away from people, in the forests, mountains, plains, etc.

Domesticated animals work for people or live with them.

Share your answers.

1. Do you have any pets? any farm animals?

2. Which of these animals are in your neighborhood? Which are not?

1. **moose**
   麋鹿

2. **mountain lion**
   山獅

3. **coyote**
   山狗

4. **opossum**
   負鼠

5. **wolf**
   狼

6. **buffalo/bison**
   水牛／美洲野牛

7. **bat**
   蝙蝠

8. **armadillo**
   犰狳

9. **beaver**
   海狸

10. **porcupine**
    豪豬

11. **bear**
    熊

12. **skunk**
    臭鼬

13. **raccoon**
    浣熊

14. **deer**
    鹿

15. **fox**
    狐狸

16. **antler**
    鹿角

17. **hoof**
    蹄

18. **whiskers**
    鬚

19. **coat/fur**
    皮／毛

20. **paw**
    腳爪

21. **horn**
    角

22. **tail**
    尾巴

23. **quill**
    羽毛

  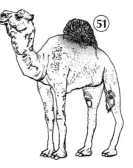

24. anteater
食蟻獸

25. leopard
豹

26. llama
駱馬

27. monkey
猴

28. chimpanzee
黑猩猩

29. rhinoceros
犀牛

30. gorilla
大猩猩

31. hyena
土狼

32. baboon
狒狒

33. giraffe
長頸鹿

34. zebra
斑馬

35. antelope
羚羊

36. lion
獅子

37. tiger
老虎

38. camel
駱駝

39. panther
黑豹

40. orangutan
猩猩

41. panda
熊貓

42. elephant
大象

43. hippopotamus
河馬

44. kangaroo
袋鼠

45. koala
無尾熊

46. platypus
鴨嘴獸

47. trunk
象鼻

48. tusk
長牙

49. mane
鬃

50. pouch
肚袋

51. hump
駝峰

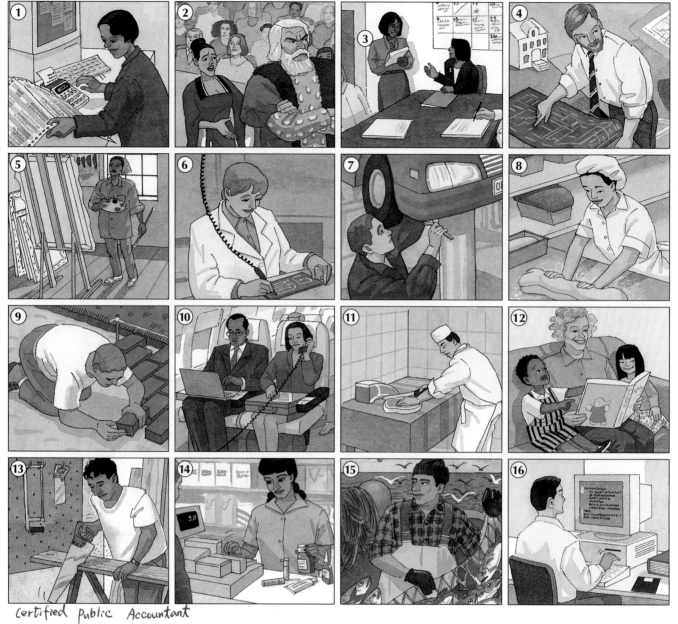

Certified public Accountant

1. accountant = c. p. A.
會計師

2. actor
演員

3. administrative assistant
行政助理

4. architect
建築師

5. artist
藝術家

6. assembler
裝配員

7. auto mechanic
汽車技工

8. baker
麵包師傅

9. bricklayer
砌磚工人

10. businessman/businesswoman
商人／女商人

11. butcher
屠夫

12. caregiver/baby-sitter
保姆

13. carpenter
木工

14. cashier
收銀員

15. commercial fisher
捕魚為業的人

16. computer programmer
電腦程式設計師

Use the new language.

1. Who works outside?

2. Who works inside?

3. Who makes things?

4. Who uses a computer?

5. Who wears a uniform?

6. Who sells things?

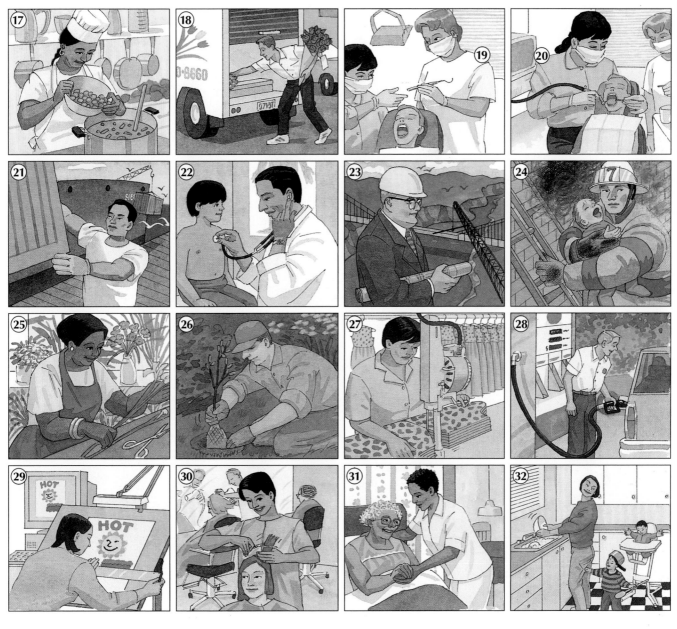

17. cook
廚師

18. delivery person
送貨員

19. dental assistant
牙醫助理

20. dentist
牙醫

21. dockworker
碼頭工人

22. doctor
醫生

23. engineer
工程師

24. firefighter
消防隊員

25. florist
花商

26. gardener
園丁

27. garment worker
衣服縫製工

28. gas station attendant
加油站服務員

29. graphic artist
美術設計員

30. hairdresser
美髮師

31. home attendant 照顧.看護
家庭看護

32. homemaker
家庭主婦

Share your answers.

1. Do you know people who have some of these jobs?
What do they say about their work?

2. Which of these jobs are available in your city?

3. For which of these jobs do you need special training?

33. housekeeper =
管家 房務員

34. <u>interpreter</u>/translator
口譯員／<u>筆譯</u>員

35. <u>janitor</u>/<u>custodian</u>
工友／管理員

36. lawyer = attorny
律師

37. machine operator
機器操作員

38. messenger/<u>courier</u>
傳信者／送信者

39. model
模特兒

40. mover
搬運工人

41. musician
音樂家

42. nurse
護士

43. painter
畫家

44. police officer = cop
警察

45. postal worker
郵務員

46. printer
印刷工

47. receptionist
招待員

48. repair person
修理工

Talk about each of the jobs or occupations.

She's a <u>housekeeper</u>. She works in <u>a hotel</u>.
He's <u>an interpreter</u>. He works for <u>the government</u>.

She's <u>a nurse</u>. She works with <u>patients</u>.

49. reporter
記者

50. salesclerk / salesperson
銷售員／推銷員

51. sanitation worker
環境衛生工作人員

52. secretary
秘書

53. server
侍者

54. serviceman / servicewoman
男軍人／女軍人

55. stock clerk
庫存職員

56. store owner
店主

57. student
學生

58. teacher / instructor
老師／教師

59. telemarketer
電話行銷員

60. travel agent
旅行業者

61. truck driver
卡車司機

62. veterinarian
獸醫

63. welder
焊工

64. writer / author
作家／作者

Talk about your job or the job you want.

What do you do?

　I'm a salesclerk. I work in a store.

What do you want to do?

　I want to be a veterinarian. I want to work with animals.

A. **assemble** components
装配部件

B. **assist** medical patients
協助病人

C. **cook**
烹調

D. **do** manual labor
從事勞力工作

E. **drive** a truck
開卡車

F. **operate** heavy machinery
操縱重型機械

G. **repair** appliances
修理器具

H. **sell** cars
銷售汽車

I. **sew** clothes
縫製衣服

J. **speak** another language
説另一種語言

K. **supervise** people
監管員工

L. **take care** of children
照顧孩童

M. **type**
打字

N. **use** a cash register
使用收銀機

O. **wait on** customers
服侍顧客

P. **work** on a computer
從事電腦工作

More vocabulary

act: to perform in a play, movie, or TV show

fly: to pilot an airplane

teach: to instruct, to show how to do something

Share your answers.

1. What job skills do you have? Where did you learn them?

2. What job skills do you want to learn?

A. **talk** to friends
詢問朋友

B. **look** at a job board
看工作佈告欄

C. **look** for a help wanted sign
尋找求職招示

D. **look** in the classifieds
看求職廣告

E. **call** for information
打電話取得資訊

F. **ask** about the hours
詢問工作時間

G. **fill out** an application
填寫申請表

H. **go** on an interview
進行面試

I. **talk** about your experience
談論您的經驗

J. **ask** about benefits
詢問有關工作福利

K. **inquire** about the salary
詢問薪資

L. **get hired**
獲得任用

1. desk
   桌子

2. typewriter
   打字員

3. secretary
   秘書

4. microcassette transcriber
   錄音帶聽寫員

5. stacking tray
   文件置放分層架

6. desk calendar
   桌曆

7. desk pad
   桌墊

8. calculator
   計算機

9. electric pencil sharpener
   電動削鉛筆機

10. file cabinet
    檔案櫃

11. file folder
    檔案夾

12. file clerk
    檔案管理員

13. supply cabinet
    文具櫃

14. photocopier
    影印機

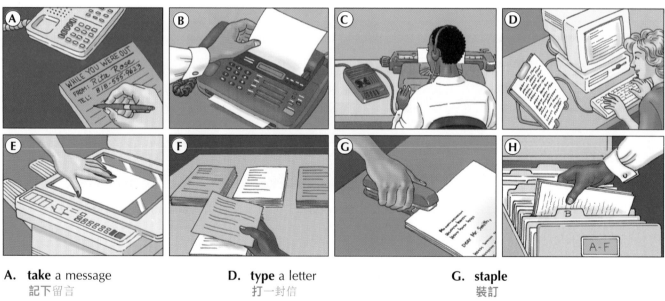

A. **take** a message
   記下留言

B. **fax** a letter
   傳真信函

C. **transcribe** notes
   抄寫筆記

D. **type** a letter
   打一封信

E. **make** copies
   複印

F. **collate** papers
   分揀文件

G. **staple**
   裝訂

H. **file** papers
   文件歸檔

Practice taking messages.

Hello. My name is <u>Sara Scott</u>. Is <u>Mr. Lee</u> in?

   Not yet. Would you like to leave a message?

Yes. Please ask <u>him</u> to call me at <u>555-4859</u>.

Share your answers.

1. Which office equipment do you know how to use?

2. Which jobs does a file clerk do?

3. Which jobs does a secretary do?

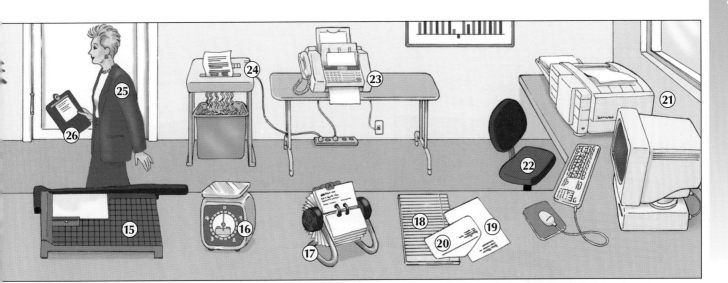

15. paper cutter
切紙刀

16. postal scale
郵件秤

17. rotary card file
筒狀型旋轉地址錄

18. legal pad
長型雜記本

19. letterhead paper
印有名字地址的信箋

20. envelope
信封

21. computer workstation
電腦專用書桌

22. swivel chair
旋轉椅

23. fax machine
傳真機

24. paper shredder
碎紙機

25. office manager
辦公室經理

26. clipboard
夾式書寫板

27. appointment book
行事曆

28. stapler
訂書機

29. staple
訂書針

30. organizer
文具盒

31. typewriter cartridge
打字機色帶

32. mailer
郵件寄發機

33. correction fluid
修正液

34. Post-it notes
可黏性便條

35. label
標籤

36. notepad
便條本

37. glue
膠水

38. rubber cement
黏膠

39. clear tape
透明膠帶

40. rubber stamp
橡皮章

41. ink pad
印台

42. packing tape
包裝用膠帶

43. pushpin
大頭釘

44. paper clip
迴紋針

45. rubber band
橡皮筋

Use the new language.

1. Which items keep things together?

2. Which items are used to mail packages?

3. Which items are made of paper?

Share your answers.

1. Which office supplies do students use?

2. Where can you buy them?

Hardware
硬體

1. **CPU** (central processing unit)
   中央處理機
2. **CD-ROM disc**
   光碟片
3. **disk drive**
   磁碟驅動器
4. **power switch**
   電源開關
5. **disk / floppy**
   磁碟片
6. **monitor / screen**
   螢幕
7. **keyboard**
   鍵盤

8. **mouse**
   滑鼠
9. **joystick**
   操縱桿
10. **surge protector**
    電壓保護器
11. **modem**
    數據機（魔電）
12. **printer**
    印表機
13. **scanner**
    掃描器
14. **laptop**
    手提電腦
15. **trackball**
    追蹤球

16. **cable**
    電纜
17. **port**
    埠
18. **motherboard**
    母板
19. **slot**
    插口
20. **hard disk drive**
    硬碟驅動器

Software
軟體

21. **program / application**
    程式／應用程式
22. **user's manual**
    使用手冊

More vocabulary

data: information that a computer can read

memory: how much data a computer can hold

speed: how fast a computer can work with data

Share your answers.

1. Can you use a computer?

2. How did you learn? in school? from a book? by yourself?

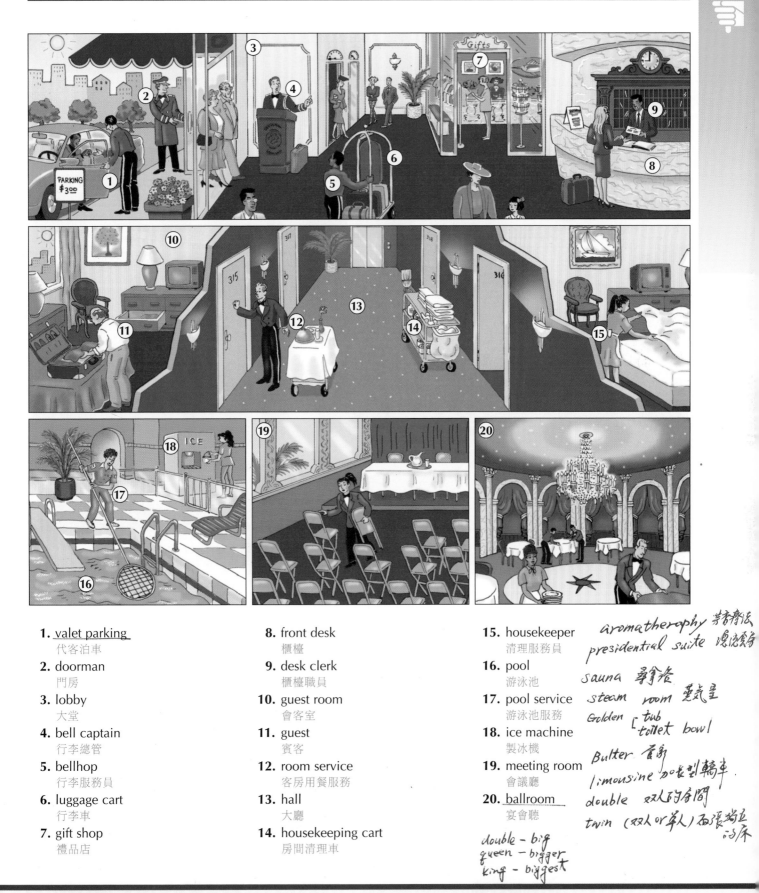

1. valet parking
代客泊車

2. doorman
門房

3. lobby
大堂

4. bell captain
行李總管

5. bellhop
行李服務員

6. luggage cart
行李車

7. gift shop
禮品店

8. front desk
櫃檯

9. desk clerk
櫃檯職員

10. guest room
會客室

11. guest
賓客

12. room service
客房用餐服務

13. hall
大廳

14. housekeeping cart
房間清理車

15. housekeeper
清理服務員

16. pool
游泳池

17. pool service
游泳池服務

18. ice machine
製冰機

19. meeting room
會議廳

20. ballroom
宴會聽

aromatherapy 芳香療法
presidential suite 總流房

sauna 争拿套
steam room 热气室
Golden [*tub*
[*toilet bowl*

Butler 音新
limousine 加長到轎車
double 双人的房間
twin (双人or单人) 两張獨立的床

double – big
queen – bigger
king – biggest

More vocabulary

concierge: the hotel worker who helps guests find restaurants and interesting places to go 服務中心
service elevator: an elevator for hotel workers

Share your answers.

1. Does this look like a hotel in your city? Which one?

2. Which hotel job is the most difficult?

3. How much does it cost to stay in a hotel in your city?

1. front office
   辦公處

2. factory owner
   工廠老闆

3. designer
   設計師

4. time clock
   打卡機

5. line supervisor
   裝配線監工

6. factory worker
   工廠工人

7. parts
   零件

8. assembly line
   裝配線

9. warehouse
   倉庫

10. order puller
    供貨員

11. hand truck
    手操縱平台車

12. conveyor belt
    傳送帶

13. packer
    包裝工人

14. forklift
    叉式起重車

15. shipping clerk
    負責裝運職員

16. loading dock
    卸載平台

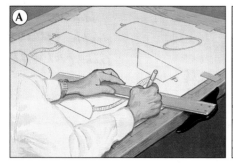

A. **design**
   設計

B. **manufacture**
   製作

C. **ship**
   裝運

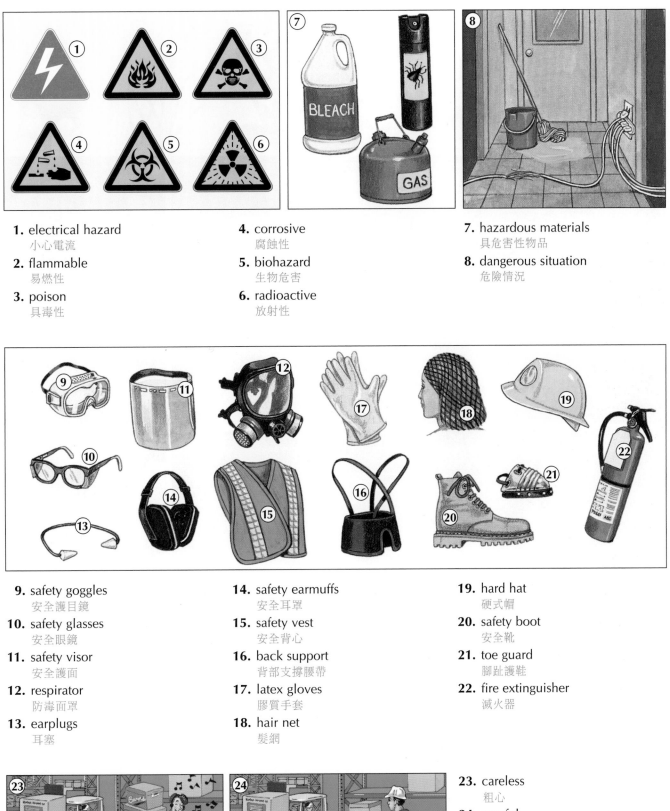

1. electrical hazard
   小心電流

2. flammable
   易燃性

3. poison
   具毒性

4. corrosive
   腐蝕性

5. biohazard
   生物危害

6. radioactive
   放射性

7. hazardous materials
   具危害性物品

8. dangerous situation
   危險情況

9. safety goggles
   安全護目鏡

10. safety glasses
    安全眼鏡

11. safety visor
    安全護面

12. respirator
    防毒面罩

13. earplugs
    耳塞

14. safety earmuffs
    安全耳罩

15. safety vest
    安全背心

16. back support
    背部支撐腰帶

17. latex gloves
    膠質手套

18. hair net
    髮網

19. hard hat
    硬式帽

20. safety boot
    安全靴

21. toe guard
    腳趾護鞋

22. fire extinguisher
    滅火器

23. careless
    粗心

24. careful
    小心

Crops
農作物

1. rice
稻米

2. wheat
小麥

3. soybeans
黃豆

4. corn
玉米

5. alfalfa
苜蓿芽

6. cotton
棉花

7. field
農田

8. farmworker
農場工人

9. tractor
拖拉機

10. farm equipment
農場設備

11. barn
穀倉

12. vegetable garden
菜園

13. livestock
牲畜

14. vineyard
葡萄園

15. farmer / grower
農夫／種植者

16. orchard
果園

17. corral
畜欄

18. hay
乾草

19. fence
柵欄

20. hired hand
幫手

21. steers / cattle
犍牛／牛

22. rancher
農場工人

A. plant
種植

B. harvest
收割

C. milk
擠牛奶

D. feed
餵養

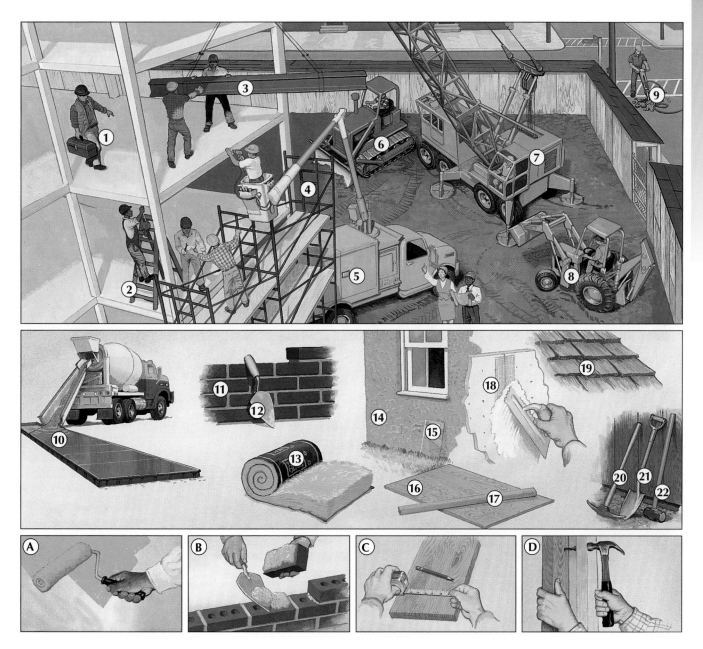

1. construction worker
   建築工人

2. ladder
   梯子

3. I beam／girder
   柱／樑

4. scaffolding
   支架

5. cherry picker
   車載升降台

6. bulldozer
   推土機

7. crane
   吊車

8. backhoe
   反向鏟挖土機

9. jackhammer／pneumatic drill
   手持式鑿岩機／風鑽台

10. concrete
    水泥

11. bricks
    磚塊

12. trowel
    泥刀

13. insulation
    隔熱層

14. stucco
    灰泥

15. window pane
    窗玻璃

16. plywood
    三夾板

17. wood／lumber
    木材／木條板

18. drywall
    清水牆

19. shingles
    木片瓦

20. pickax
    鶴嘴鋤

21. shovel
    鐵鍬

22. sledgehammer
    大鎚

A. **paint**
   上油漆

B. **lay** bricks
   砌磚塊

C. **measure**
   測量

D. **hammer**
   釘鎚

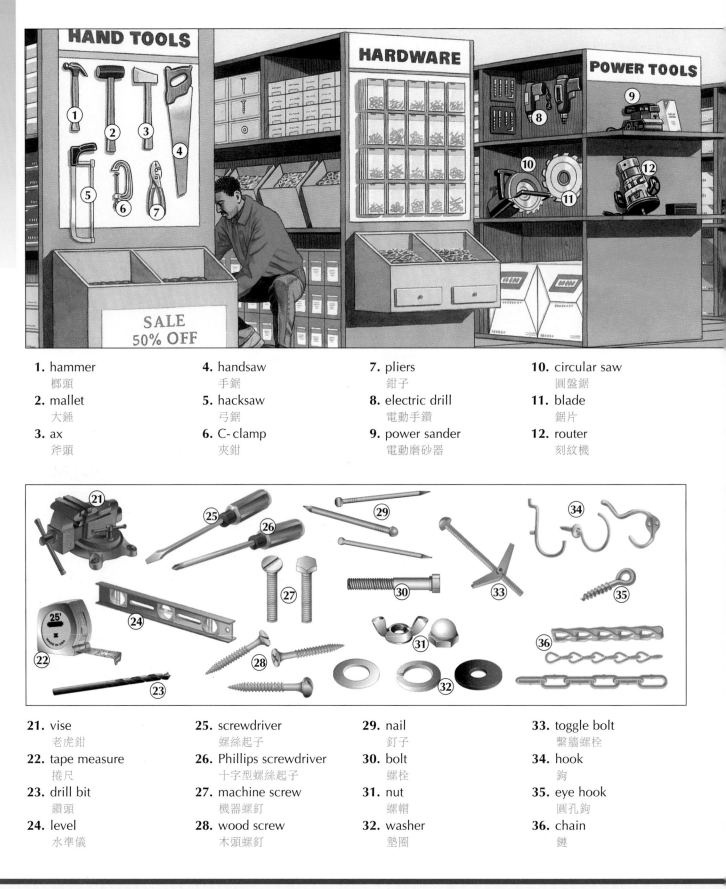

1. hammer
槌頭

2. mallet
大鎚

3. ax
斧頭

4. handsaw
手鋸

5. hacksaw
弓鋸

6. C-clamp
夾鉗

7. pliers
鉗子

8. electric drill
電動手鑽

9. power sander
電動磨砂器

10. circular saw
圓盤鋸

11. blade
鋸片

12. router
刻紋機

21. vise
老虎鉗

22. tape measure
捲尺

23. drill bit
鑽頭

24. level
水準儀

25. screwdriver
螺絲起子

26. Phillips screwdriver
十字型螺絲起子

27. machine screw
機器螺釘

28. wood screw
木頭螺釘

29. nail
釘子

30. bolt
螺栓

31. nut
螺帽

32. washer
墊圈

33. toggle bolt
繫牆螺栓

34. hook
鉤

35. eye hook
圓孔鉤

36. chain
鏈

Use the new language.

1. Which tools are used for plumbing?

2. Which tools are used for painting?

3. Which tools are used for electrical work?

4. Which tools are used for working with wood?

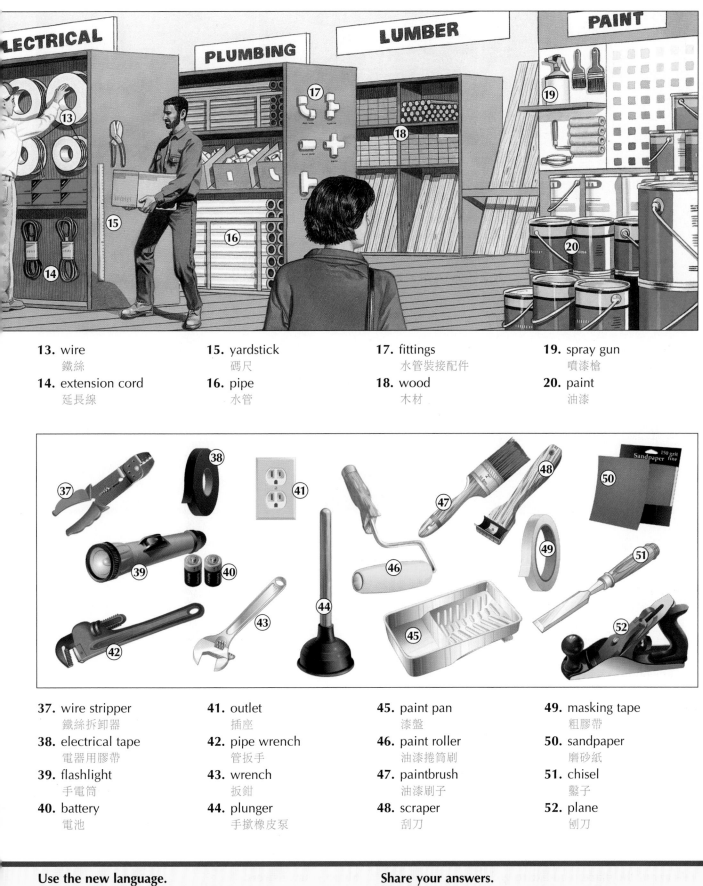

13. wire
鐵絲

14. extension cord
延長線

15. yardstick
碼尺

16. pipe
水管

17. fittings
水管裝接配件

18. wood
木材

19. spray gun
噴漆槍

20. paint
油漆

37. wire stripper
鐵絲拆卸器

38. electrical tape
電器用膠帶

39. flashlight
手電筒

40. battery
電池

41. outlet
插座

42. pipe wrench
管扳手

43. wrench
扳鉗

44. plunger
手撳橡皮泵

45. paint pan
漆盤

46. paint roller
油漆捲筒刷

47. paintbrush
油漆刷子

48. scraper
刮刀

49. masking tape
粗膠帶

50. sandpaper
磨砂紙

51. chisel
鑿子

52. plane
刨刀

Use the new language.

Look at **Household Problems and Repairs,**
pages **48–49.**

Name the tools you use to fix the problems you see.

Share your answers.

1. Which tools do you have in your home?

2. Which tools can be dangerous to use?

1. zoo
   動物園
2. animals
   動物
3. zookeeper
   動物管理員
4. botanical gardens
   植物園
5. greenhouse
   溫室
6. gardener
   園丁
7. art museum
   美術館
8. painting
   畫
9. sculpture
   雕像

10. the movies
    電影
11. seat
    座椅
12. screen
    螢幕
13. amusement park
    遊樂園
14. puppet show
    布偶表演
15. roller coaster
    雲霄飛車
16. carnival
    嘉年華會
17. rides
    騎旋轉木馬
18. game
    遊戲

19. county fair
    市集
20. first place/first prize
    第一名／特獎
21. exhibition
    展示
22. swap meet/flea market
    市集／跳蚤市場
23. booth
    攤位
24. merchandise
    商品
25. baseball game
    棒球比賽
26. stadium
    運動場
27. announcer
    播報員

Talk about the places you like to go.

I like <u>animals</u>, so I go to <u>the zoo</u>.

I like <u>rides</u>, so I go to <u>carnivals</u>.

Share your answers.

1. Which of these places is interesting to you?
2. Which rides do you like at an amusement park?
3. What are some famous places to go to in your country?

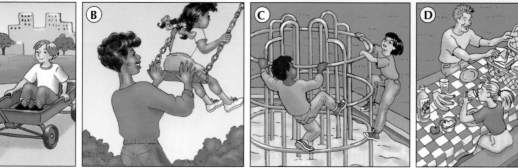

1. ball field 球場	**8.** picnic table 野餐桌	**15.** sandbox 沙坑
2. bike path 自行車道	**9.** tricycle 三輪車	**16.** seesaw 蹺蹺板
3. cyclist 騎自行車的人	**10.** bench 長板凳	**A.** **pull** the wagon 拉四輪車
4. bicycle/bike 自行車	**11.** water fountain 噴水池	**B.** **push** the swing 推鞦韆
5. jump rope 跳繩	**12.** swings 鞦韆	**C.** **climb** on the bars 爬單槓
6. duck pond 鴨池	**13.** slide 溜滑梯	**D.** **picnic/have** a picnic 野餐
7. tennis court 網球場	**14.** climbing apparatus 攀爬設施	

1. camping
露營

2. boating
划船

3. canoeing
划獨木舟

4. rafting
泛舟

5. fishing
釣魚

6. hiking
健行

7. backpacking
野外行走

8. mountain biking
騎越野自行車

9. horseback riding
騎馬

10. tent
帳篷

11. campfire
營火

12. sleeping bag
睡袋

13. foam pad
泡沫墊

14. life vest
救生背心

15. backpack
背包

16. camping stove
野營用火爐

17. fishing net
魚網

18. fishing pole
魚桿

19. rope
麻繩

20. multi-use knife
多用途小刀

21. matches
火柴

22. lantern
燈籠

23. insect repellent
驅蟲劑

24. canteen
水壺

1. ocean/water
   海洋／海水

2. fins
   蛙鞋

3. diving mask
   潛水面罩

4. sailboat
   帆船

5. surfboard
   衝浪板

6. wave
   波浪

7. wet suit
   潛水衣

8. scuba tank
   水下呼吸筒

9. beach umbrella
   海灘遮陽傘

10. sand castle
    沙堡

11. cooler
    保溫箱

12. shade
    蔭涼

13. sunscreen/sunblock
    防曬油

14. beach chair
    海灘椅

15. beach towel
    海灘巾

16. pier
    碼頭

17. sunbather
    作日光浴的人

18. lifeguard
    救生員

19. life saving device
    救生設備

20. lifeguard station
    救生站

21. seashell
    貝殼

22. pail/bucket
    水桶

23. sand
    沙

24. rock
    岩石

More vocabulary

seaweed: a plant that grows in the ocean

tide: the level of the ocean. The tide goes in and out every twelve hours.

Share your answers.

1. Are there any beaches near your home?

2. Do you prefer to spend more time on the sand or in the water?

3. Where are some of the world's best beaches?

A. **walk**
   走路

B. **jog**
   慢跑

C. **run**
   跑步

D. **throw**
   丟擲

E. **catch**
   接

F. **pitch**
   投

G. **hit**
   打擊

H. **pass**
   傳球

I. **shoot**
   射

J. **jump**
   跳

K. **dribble / bounce**
   運球／拍球

L. **kick**
   踢

M. **tackle**
   擒抱

Practice talking about what you can do.

I can <u>swim</u>, but I can't <u>dive</u>.

I can <u>pass the ball</u> well, but I can't <u>shoot</u> too well.

Use the new language.

Look at **Individual Sports**, page **159**.

Name the actions you see people doing.

The man in number 18 is riding a horse.

N.	serve 發球	R.	bend 彎腰	V.	skate 溜冰	Z.	finish 跑到終點
O.	swing 揮球	S.	dive 跳水	W.	ride 騎		
P.	exercise / work out 運動	T.	swim 游泳	X.	start 起跑		
Q.	stretch 伸拉	U.	ski 滑雪	Y.	race 賽跑		

Share your answers.

1. What do you like to do?

2. What do you have difficulty doing?

3. How often do you exercise? Once a week? Two or three times a week? More? Never?

4. Which is more difficult, throwing a ball or catching it?

1. score
分數

2. coach
教練

3. team
團隊

4. fan
球迷

5. player
球員

6. official / referee
裁判

7. basketball court
籃球場

8. basketball
籃球

9. baseball
棒球

10. softball
壘球

11. football
橄欖球

12. soccer
足球

13. ice hockey
冰上曲棍球

14. volleyball
排球

15. water polo
水球

More vocabulary

captain: the team leader

umpire: in baseball, the name for referee

Little League: a baseball league for children

win: to have the best score

lose: the opposite of win

tie: to have the same score as the other team

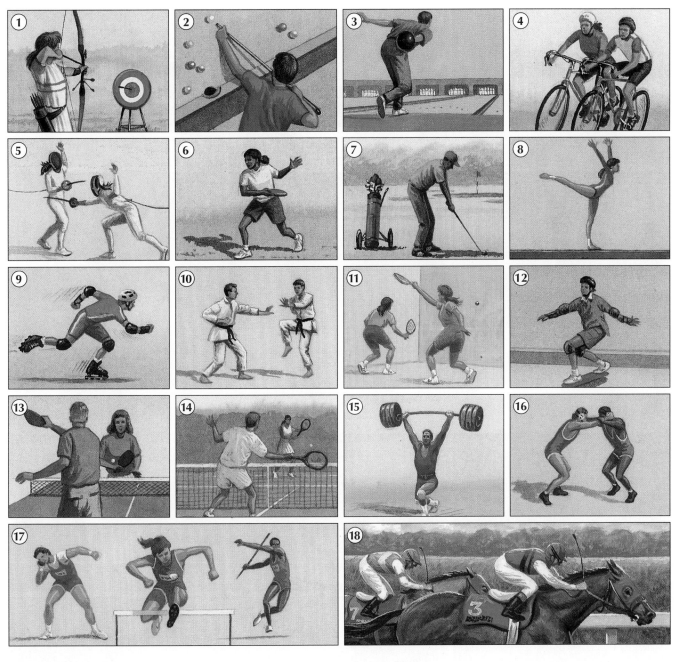

1. archery
   射箭

2. billiards/pool
   撞球

3. bowling
   保齡球

4. cycling/biking
   騎車

5. fencing
   劍擊

6. flying disc*
   飛盤

7. golf
   高爾夫球

8. gymnastics
   體操

9. inline skating
   滑單排輪鞋

10. martial arts
    武術

11. racquetball
    回力球

12. skateboarding
    溜滑板

13. table tennis/
    Ping-Pong™
    乒乓球

14. tennis
    網球

15. weightlifting
    舉重

16. wrestling
    角力

17. track and field
    田徑

18. horse racing
    賽馬

*Note: One brand is Frisbee®
(Mattel, Inc.)

Talk about sports.

Which sports do you like?

I like tennis but I don't like golf.

Share your answers.

1. Which sports are good for children to learn? Why?

2. Which sport is the most difficult to learn? Why?

3. Which sport is the most dangerous? Why?

1. downhill skiing
下坡滑雪

2. snowboarding
滑雪板

3. cross-country skiing
越野滑雪

4. ice skating
溜冰

5. figure skating
花式溜冰

6. sledding
滑雪橇

7. waterskiing
滑水

8. sailing
玩風帆

9. surfing
衝浪

10. sailboarding
坐滑浪板

11. snorkeling
潛泳

12. scuba diving
潛水

Use the new language.

Look at **The Beach**, page 155.

Name the sports you see.

Share your answers.

1. Which sports are in the Winter Olympics?

2. Which sports do you think are the most exciting to watch?

1. **golf club**
高爾夫球桿

2. **tennis racket**
網球拍

3. **volleyball**
排球

4. **basketball**
籃球

5. **bowling ball**
保齡球

6. **bow**
弓

7. **arrow**
箭

8. **target**
箭靶

9. **ice skates**
冰鞋

10. **inline skates**
單排輪鞋

11. **hockey stick**
曲棍

12. **soccer ball**
足球

13. **shin guards**
脛護墊

14. **baseball bat**
球棒

15. **catcher's mask**
捕手面罩

16. **uniform**
制服

17. **glove**
手套

18. **baseball**
棒球

19. **weights**
舉重

20. **football helmet**
橄欖球頭盔

21. **shoulder pads**
肩墊

22. **football**
橄欖球

23. **snowboard**
雪板

24. **skis**
滑雪展

25. **ski poles**
滑雪杖

26. **ski boots**
滑雪靴

27. **flying disc***
飛盤

*Note: One brand is Frisbee®
(Mattel, Inc.)

Share your answers.

1. Which sports equipment is used for safety reasons?

2. Which sports equipment is heavy?

3. What sports equipment do you have at home?

Use the new language.

Look at **Individual Sports,** page **159.**

Name the sports equipment you see.

A. collect things
收集東西

B. play games
玩遊戲

C. build models
造模型

D. do crafts
做手工藝品

1. video game system
   電視遊樂器系統

2. cartridge
   遊樂器帶

3. board game
   棋盤遊戲

4. dice
   骰子

5. checkers
   西洋跳棋

6. chess
   西洋棋

7. model kit
   模型組合

8. glue
   膠水

9. acrylic paint
   壓克力漆

10. figurine
    小雕像

11. baseball card
    棒球卡

12. stamp collection
    集郵

13. coin collection
    集錢幣

14. clay
    黏土

15. doll making kit
    娃娃製作組合

16. woodworking kit
    木工組合

Talk about how much time you spend on your hobbies.

I *do crafts* all the time.

I *play chess* sometimes.

I never *build models*.

Share your answers.

1. How often do you play video games? Often? Sometimes? Never?

2. What board games do you know?

3. Do you collect anything? What?

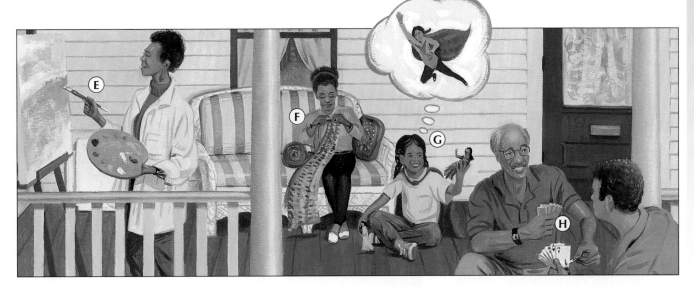

E. paint
上油漆

F. knit
編織

G. pretend
模仿假裝

H. play cards
玩牌

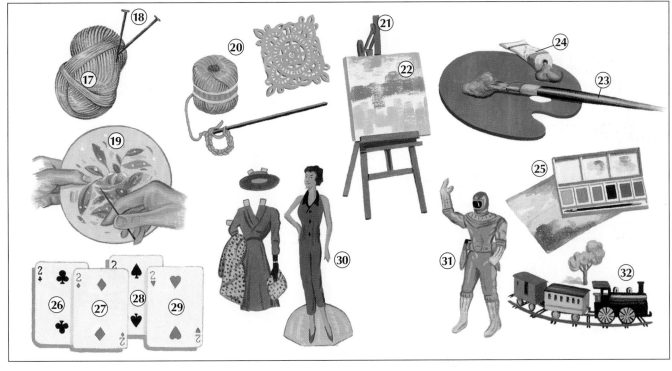

17. yarn
紗線

18. knitting needles
織針

19. embroidery
刺繡

20. crochet
鉤針

21. easel
畫架

22. canvas
畫布

23. paintbrush
畫筆

24. oil paint
油畫

25. watercolor
水彩

26. clubs
黑梅花

27. diamonds
方塊

28. spades
黑桃

29. hearts
紅心

30. paper doll
紙娃娃

31. action figure
動作人物

32. model trains
模型火車

Share your answers.

1. Do you like to play cards? Which games?

2. Did you pretend a lot when you were a child? What did you pretend to be?

3. Is it important to have hobbies? Why or why not?

4. What's your favorite game?

5. What's your hobby?

1. clock radio
   鬧鐘收音機
2. portable radio-cassette player
   手提收錄音機
3. cassette recorder
   錄音機
4. microphone
   麥克風
5. shortwave radio
   短波收音機
6. TV (television)
   電視機
7. portable TV
   手提電視機

8. VCR (videocassette recorder)
   錄放影機
9. remote control
   遙控器
10. videocassette
    錄影帶
11. speakers
    喇叭
12. turntable
    轉盤
13. tuner
    選台鈕
14. CD player
    CD唱盤

15. personal radio-cassette player
    個人用隨身聽
16. headphones
    耳機
17. adapter
    轉接器
18. plug
    插頭

19. video camera
    攝影機
20. tripod
    三腳架
21. camcorder
    小型攝影機
22. battery pack
    電池組
23. battery charger
    充電器
24. 35 mm camera
    35毫米照相機
25. zoom lens
    可變焦距鏡片
26. film
    軟片

27. camera case
    照相機袋盒
28. screen
    螢幕
29. carousel slide projector
    圓形幻燈片投影機
30. slide tray
    幻燈片盒
31. slides
    幻燈片
32. photo album
    相簿
33. out of focus
    失焦
34. overexposed
    曝光過度

35. underexposed
    曝光不夠
A. **record**
    錄
B. **play**
    放
C. **fast forward**
    快轉
D. **rewind**
    迴轉
E. **pause**
    暫停
F. **stop** and **eject**
    停止、取帶

Types of entertainment 娛樂種類

1. film/movie
電影

2. play
舞台劇

3. television program
電視節目

4. radio program
收音機節目

5. stand-up comedy
單口相聲

6. concert
音樂會

7. ballet
芭蕾

8. opera
歌劇

Types of stories 劇情種類

9. western
西部片

10. comedy
喜劇

11. tragedy
悲劇

12. science fiction story
科幻片

13. action story/
adventure story
動作／冒險片

14. horror story
恐怖片

15. mystery
懸疑片

16. romance
愛情片

Types of TV programs　電視節目種類

17. news
新聞

18. sitcom (situation comedy)
情境喜劇片、影集

19. cartoon
卡通

20. talk show
脫口秀

21. soap opera
連續劇

22. nature program
大自然節目

23. game show/quiz show
遊戲節目／益智節目

24. children's program
兒童節目

25. shopping program
購物節目

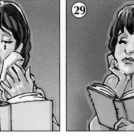

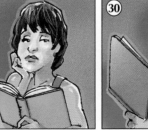

26. serious book
讓人感到**嚴肅**的書

28. sad book
讓人**感傷**的書

30. interesting book
讓人感到**有趣**的書

27. funny book
讓人**發笑**的書

29. boring book
讓人**無聊**的書

1. New Year's Day
   元旦
2. parade
   遊行
3. confetti
   五彩碎紙
4. Valentine's Day
   情人節
5. card
   卡片
6. heart
   紅心
7. Independence Day / 4th of July
   獨立紀念日／七月四日

8. fireworks
   煙火
9. flag
   國旗
10. Halloween
    萬聖節
11. jack-o'-lantern
    南瓜人面形燈籠
12. mask
    面具
13. costume
    服裝
14. candy
    糖果

15. Thanksgiving
    感恩節
16. feast
    盛宴
17. turkey
    火雞
18. Christmas
    聖誕節
19. ornament
    掛飾品
20. Christmas tree
    聖誕樹

A. **plan** a party
計畫派對

B. **invite** the guests
邀請客人

C. **decorate** the house
佈置房子

D. **wrap** a gift
包裝禮物

E. **hide**
藏

F. **answer** the door
應門

G. **shout** "surprise!"
叫 "驚喜！"

H. **light** the candles
點蠟燭

I. **sing** "Happy Birthday"
唱 "生日快樂" 歌

J. **make** a wish
許願

K. **blow out** the candles
吹熄蠟燭

L. **open** the presents
打開禮物

Practice inviting friends to a party.

I'd love for you to come to my party <u>next week</u>.

Could <u>you and your friend</u> come to my party?

Would <u>your friend</u> like to come to a party I'm giving?

Share your answers.

1. Do you celebrate birthdays? What do you do?

2. Are there birthdays you celebrate in a special way?

3. Is there a special birthday song in your country?

Verb Guide

Verbs in English are either regular or irregular in the past tense and past participle forms.

Regular Verbs

The regular verbs below are marked 1, 2, 3, or 4 according to four different spelling patterns.
(See page 172 for the **irregular verbs** which do not follow any of these patterns.)

Spelling Patterns for the Past and the Past Participle	*Example*		
1. Add **-ed** to the end of the verb.	**ASK**	→	**ASKED**
2. Add **-d** to the end of the verb.	**LIVE**	→	**LIVED**
3. Double the final consonant and add **-ed** to the end of the verb.	**DROP**	→	**DROPPED**
4. Drop the final y and add **-ied** to the end of the verb.	**CRY**	→	**CRIED**

The Oxford Picture Dictionary List of Regular Verbs

act (1)
add (1)
address (1)
answer (1)
apologize (2)
appear (1)
applaud (1)
arrange (2)
arrest (1)
arrive (2)
ask (1)
assemble (2)
assist (1)
bake (2)
barbecue (2)
bathe (2)
board (1)
boil (1)
borrow (1)
bounce (2)
brainstorm (1)
breathe (2)
broil (1)
brush (1)
burn (1)
call (1)
carry (4)
change (2)
check (1)
choke (2)
chop (3)
circle (2)
claim (1)
clap (3)
clean (1)
clear (1)
climb (1)
close (2)
collate (2)

collect (1)
color (1)
comb (1)
commit (3)
compliment (1)
conserve (2)
convert (1)
cook (1)
copy (4)
correct (1)
cough (1)
count (1)
cross (1)
cry (4)
dance (2)
design (1)
deposit (1)
deliver (1)
dial (1)
dictate (2)
die (2)
discuss (1)
dive (2)
dress (1)
dribble (2)
drill (1)
drop (3)
drown (1)
dry (4)
dust (1)
dye (2)
edit (1)
eject (1)
empty (4)
end (1)
enter (1)
erase (2)
examine (2)
exchange (2)

exercise (2)
experience (2)
exterminate (2)
fasten (1)
fax (1)
file (2)
fill (1)
finish (1)
fix (1)
floss (1)
fold (1)
fry (4)
gargle (2)
graduate (2)
grate (2)
grease (2)
greet (1)
grill (1)
hail (1)
hammer (1)
harvest (1)
help (1)
hire (2)
hug (3)
immigrate (2)
inquire (2)
insert (1)
introduce (2)
invite (2)
iron (1)
jog (3)
join (1)
jump (1)
kick (1)
kiss (1)
knit (3)
land (1)
laugh (1)
learn (1)

lengthen (1)
listen (1)
live (2)
load (1)
lock (1)
look (1)
mail (1)
manufacture (2)
mark (1)
match (1)
measure (2)
milk (1)
miss (1)
mix (1)
mop (3)
move (2)
mow (1)
need (1)
nurse (2)
obey (1)
observe (2)
open (1)
operate (2)
order (1)
overdose (2)
paint (1)
park (1)
pass (1)
pause (2)
peel (1)
perm (1)
pick (1)
pitch (1)
plan (3)
plant (1)
play (1)
point (1)
polish (1)
pour (1)
pretend (1)
print (1)
protect (1)

pull (1)
push (1)
race (2)
raise (2)
rake (2)
receive (2)
record (1)
recycle (2)
register (1)
relax (1)
remove (2)
rent (1)
repair (1)
repeat (1)
report (1)
request (1)
return (1)
rinse (2)
roast (1)
rock (1)
sauté (2)
save (2)
scrub (3)
seat (1)
sentence (2)
serve (2)
share (2)
shave (2)
ship (3)
shop (3)
shorten (1)
shout (1)
sign (1)
simmer (1)
skate (2)
ski (1)
slice (2)
smell (1)
sneeze (2)
sort (1)
spell (1)
staple (2)

start (1)
stay (1)
steam (1)
stir (3)
stir-fry (4)
stop (3)
stow (1)
stretch (1)
supervise (2)
swallow (1)
tackle (2)
talk (1)
taste (2)
thank (1)
tie (2)
touch (1)
transcribe (2)
transfer (3)
travel (1)
trim (3)
turn (1)
type (2)
underline (2)
unload (1)
unpack (1)
use (2)
vacuum (1)
vomit (1)
vote (2)
wait (1)
walk (1)
wash (1)
watch (1)
water (1)
weed (1)
weigh (1)
wipe (2)
work (1)
wrap (3)
yield (1)

Verb Guide

Irregular Verbs

These verbs have irregular endings in the past and/or the past participle.

The Oxford Picture Dictionary List of Irregular Verbs

simple	past	past participle	simple	past	past participle
be	was	been	leave	left	left
beat	beat	beaten	lend	lent	lent
become	became	become	let	let	let
begin	began	begun	light	lit	lit
bend	bent	bent	make	made	made
bleed	bled	bled	pay	paid	paid
blow	blew	blown	picnic	picnicked	picnicked
break	broke	broken	put	put	put
build	built	built	read	read	read
buy	bought	bought	rewind	rewound	rewound
catch	caught	caught	rewrite	rewrote	rewritten
come	came	come	ride	rode	ridden
cut	cut	cut	run	ran	run
do	did	done	say	said	said
draw	drew	drawn	see	saw	seen
drink	drank	drunk	sell	sold	sold
drive	drove	driven	send	sent	sent
eat	ate	eaten	set	set	set
fall	fell	fallen	sew	sewed	sewn
feed	fed	fed	shoot	shot	shot
feel	felt	felt	sing	sang	sung
find	found	found	sit	sat	sat
fly	flew	flown	speak	spoke	spoken
get	got	gotten	stand	stood	stood
give	gave	given	sweep	swept	swept
go	went	gone	swim	swam	swum
hang	hung	hung	swing	swung	swung
have	had	had	take	took	taken
hear	heard	heard	teach	taught	taught
hide	hid	hidden	throw	threw	thrown
hit	hit	hit	wake	woke	woken
hold	held	held	wear	wore	worn
keep	kept	kept	withdraw	withdrew	withdrawn
lay	laid	laid	write	wrote	written

Index

Two numbers are shown after words in the index: the first refers to the page where the word is illustrated and the second refers to the item number of the word on that page. For example, cool [kōol] **10**-3 means that the word *cool* is item number 3 on page 10. If only the bold page number appears, then that word is part of the unit title or subtitle, or is found somewhere else on the page. A bold number followed by ✦ means the word can be found in the exercise space at the bottom of that page.

Words or combinations of words that appear in **bold** type are used as verbs or verb phrases. Words used as other parts of speech are shown in ordinary type. So, for example, **file** (in bold type) is the verb *file*, while file (in ordinary type) is the noun *file*. Words or phrases in small capital letters (for example, HOLIDAYS) form unit titles.

Phrases and other words that form combinations with an individual word entry are often listed underneath it. Rather than repeating the word each time it occurs in combination with what is listed under it, the word is replaced by three dots (...), called an ellipsis. For example, under the word *bus*, you will find ...driver and ...stop meaning *bus driver* and *bus stop*. Under the word *store* you will find shoe... and toy..., meaning *shoe store* and *toy store*.

Pronunciation Guide

The index includes a pronunciation guide for all the words and phrases illustrated in the book. This guide uses symbols commonly found in dictionaries for native speakers. These symbols, unlike those used in pronunciation systems such as the International Phonetic Alphabet, tend to use English spelling patterns and so should help you to become more aware of the connections between written English and spoken English.

Consonants

[b] as in back [băk]

[ch] as in cheek [chēk]

[d] as in date [dāt]

[dh] as in this [dhĭs]

[f] as in face [fās]

[g] as in gas [găs]

[h] as in half [hăf]

[j] as in jam [jăm]

[k] as in key [kē]

[l] as in leaf [lēf]

[m] as in match [măch]

[n] as in neck [něk]

[ng] as in ring [rĭng]

[p] as in park [pärk]

[r] as in rice [rīs]

[s] as in sand [sănd]

[sh] as in shoe [shōo]

[t] as in tape [tāp]

[th] as in three [thrē]

[v] as in vine [vīn]

[w] as in wait [wāt]

[y] as in yams [yămz]

[z] as in zoo [zōo]

[zh] as in measure [mězhʼər]

Vowels

[ā] as in bake [bāk]

[ă] as in back [băk]

[ä] as in car [kär] or box [bäks]

[ē] as in beat [bēt]

[ĕ] as in bed [bĕd] .

[ë] as in bear [bër]

[ī] as in line [līn]

[ĭ] as in lip [lĭp]

[ï] as in near [nïr]

[ō] as in cold [kōld]

[ö] as in short [shört]

    or claw [klö]

[ōo] as in cool [kōol]

[ŏo] as in cook [kŏok]

[ow] as in cow [kow]

[oy] as in boy [boy]

[ŭ] as in cut [kŭt]

[ü] as in curb [kürb]

[ə] as in above [ə bŭvʼ]

All the pronunciation symbols used are alphabetical except for the schwa [ə]. The schwa is the most frequent vowel sound in English. If you use the schwa appropriately in unstressed syllables, your pronunciation will sound more natural.

Vowels before [r] are shown with the symbol [¨] to call attention to the special quality that vowels have before [r]. (Note that the symbols [ä] and [ö] are also used for vowels not followed by [r], as in *box* or *claw*.) You should listen carefully to native speakers to discover how these vowels actually sound.

Stress

This index follows the system for marking stress used in many dictionaries for native speakers.

1. Stress is not marked if a word consisting of a single syllable occurs by itself.

2. Where stress is marked, two levels are distinguished:

a bold accent [ʼ] is placed after each syllable with primary (or strong) stress, a light accent [ʼ] is placed after each syllable with secondary (or weaker) stress.

In phrases and other combinations of words, stress is indicated for each word as it would be pronounced within the whole phrase or other unit. If a word consisting of a single syllable is stressed in the combinations listed below it, the accent mark indicating the degree of stress it has in the phrases (primary or secondary) is shown in parentheses. A hyphen replaces any part of a word or phrase that is omitted. For example, bus [bŭs(ʼ–)] shows that the word *bus* is said with primary stress in the combinations shown below it. The word ...driver [–drīʼvər], listed under *bus*, shows that *driver* has secondary stress in the combination *bus driver*: [bŭsʼ drīʼvər].

Syllable Boundaries

Syllable boundaries are indicated by a single space or by a stress mark.

Note: The pronunciations shown in this index are based on patterns of American English. There has been no attempt to represent all of the varieties of American English. Students should listen to native speakers to hear how the language actually sounds in a particular region.

Index

Index

Index

Index

Index

Index

Index

Index

Index

Geographical Index

Continents

Countries and other locations

Mongolia [mäng gō/lē ə] **124–125**
Montenegro [män/tə nē/grō, –nĕ/–] **124–125**
Morocco [mə räk/ō] **124–125**
Mozambique [mō/zəm bēk/] **124–125**
Myanmar [myän/mär/] **124–125**
Namibia [nə mĭb/ē ə] **124–125**
Nauru [nä ōō/rōō] **124–125**
Nepal [nə pöl/, –päl/] **124–125**
Netherlands [nĕdh/ər ləndz] **124–125**
New Guinea [nōō/ gĭn/ē] **124–125**
New Zealand [nōō/ zē/lənd] **124–125**
Nicaragua [nĭk/ə rä/gwə] **122–125**
Niger [nī/jər, nē zhĕr/] **124–125**
Nigeria [nī jïr/ē ə] **124–125**
North Korea [nörth/ kə rē/ə] **124–125**
Norway [nör/wā] **124–125**
Oman [ō män/] **124–125**
Pakistan [păk/ə stăn/] **124–125**
Palau [pə low/] **124–125**
Panama [păn/ə mä/] **122–125**
Papua New Guinea [păp/yōō ə nōō/ gĭn/ē] **124–125**
Paraguay [păr/ə gwī/, –gwä/] **124–125**
Peru [pə rōō/] **124–125**
Philippines [fĭl/ə pēnz/, fĭl/ə pēnz/] **124–125**
Poland [pō/lənd] **124–125**
Portugal [pör/chə gəl] **124–125**
Puerto Rico [pwĕr/tə rē/kō, pör/tə–] **122–125**
Qatar [kä/tär, kə tär/] **124–125**
Romania [rō mā/nē ə, rōō–] **124–125**
Russia [rŭsh/ə] **124–125**
Rwanda [rōō än/də] **124–125**
Saudi Arabia [sow/dē ə rā/bē ə, sö/dē–] **124–125**
Senegal [sĕn/ə göl/, –gäl/] **124–125**
Serbia [sür/bē ə] **124–125**
Seychelles [sā shĕlz/, –shĕl/] **124–125**
Sierra Leone [sē ĕr/ə lē ōn/, –lē ō/nē] **124–125**
Singapore [sĭng/ə pör/] **124–125**
Slovakia [slō vä/kē ə] **124–125**
Slovenia [slō vē/nē ə] **124–125**
Solomon Islands [säl/ə mən ī/ləndz] **124–125**
Somalia [sə mä/lē ə] **124–125**
South Africa [sowth/ ăf/rĭ kə] **124–125**
South Korea [sowth/ kə rē/ə] **124–125**
Spain [spān] **124–125**
Sri Lanka [srē/ läng/kə, shrē/–] **124–125**
Sudan [sōō dăn/] **124–125**
Sumatra [sōō mä/trə] **124–125**
Suriname [sōōr/ə nä/mə] **124–125**
Swaziland [swä/zē lănd/] **124–125**
Sweden [swēd/n] **124–125**
Switzerland [swĭt/sər lənd] **124–125**
Syria [sïr/ē ə] **124–125**
Tahiti [tə hē/tē] **124–125**
Taiwan [tī/wän/] **124–125**
Tajikistan [tä jĭk/ə stän/, –stän/] **124–125**
Tanzania [tăn/zə nē/ə] **124–125**
Tasmania [tăz mā/nē ə] **124–125**
Thailand [tī/lănd/, –lənd] **124–125**
The Gambia [dhə găm/bē ə] **124–125**
Togo [tō/gō] **124–125**
Tonga [täng/gə] **124–125**
Tunisia [tōō nē/zhə] **124–125**
Turkey [tür/kē] **124–125**
Turkmenistan [türk mĕn/ə stän/, –stän/] **124–125**
Uganda [yōō găn/də] **124–125**

Ukraine [yōō/krān, yōō krān/] **124–125**
United Arab Emirates [yōō nī/təd ăr/əb ĕm/ər əts] **124–125**
United Kingdom [yōō nī/təd kĭng/dəm] **124–125**
United States of America [yōō nī/təd stāts/ əv ə mĕr/ə kə]
   122–125
Uruguay [yōōr/ə gwī/, –gwä/] **124–125**
Uzbekistan [ōōz bĕk/ə stän/, –stän/] **124–125**
Venezuela [vĕn/ə zwā/lə] **124–125**
Vietnam [vē/ĕt näm/, –năm/] **124–125**
Western Sahara [wĕs/tərn sə hăr/ə] **124–125**
Western Samoa [wĕs/tərn sə mō/ə] **124–125**
Yemen [yĕm/ən] **124–125**
Zambia [zăm/bē ə] **124–125**
Zimbabwe [zĭm bäb/wā] **124–125**

Bodies of water

Arabian Sea [ə rā/bē ən sē/] **124–125**
Arctic Ocean [ärk/tĭk ō/shən] **122–125**
Baffin Bay [băf/ən bā/] **122–125**
Baltic Sea [böl/tĭk sē/] **124–125**
Barents Sea [băr/ənts sē/] **124–125**
Beaufort Sea [bō/fərt sē/] **122–125**
Bering Sea [bĕr/ĭng sē/, bïr/–] **122–125**
Black Sea [blăk/ sē/] **124–125**
Caribbean Sea [kăr/ə bē/ən sē/, kə rĭb/ē ən–] **122–125**
Caspian Sea [kăs/pē ən sē/] **124–125**
Coral Sea [kör/əl sē/] **124–125**
East China Sea [ēst/ chī/nə sē/] **124–125**
Greenland Sea [grēn/lənd sē/, –lănd/–] **124–125**
Gulf of Alaska [gŭlf/ əv ə lăs/kə] **122–125**
Gulf of California [gŭlf/ əv kăl/ə förn/yə] **122–125**
Gulf of Honduras [gŭlf/ əv hän dōōr/əs] **122–125**
Gulf of Mexico [gŭlf/ əv mĕk/sĭ kō/] **122–125**
Gulf of St. Lawrence [gŭlf/ əv sänt/ lör/əns, –lär/–] **122–125**
Hudson Bay [hŭd/sən bā/] **122–125**
Indian Ocean [ĭn/dē ən ō/shən] **124–125**
Labrador Sea [lăb/rə dör/ sē/] **122–125**
Mediterranean Sea [mĕd/ə tə rā/nē ən sē/] **124–125**
North Atlantic Ocean [nörth/ ət lăn/tĭk ō/shən] **122–125**
North Pacific Ocean [nörth/ pə sĭf/ĭk ō/shən] **122–125**
North Sea [nörth/ sē/] **124–125**
Norwegian Sea [nör wē/jən sē/] **124–125**
Persian Gulf [pür/zhən gŭlf/] **124–125**
Philippine Sea [fĭl/ə pēn/ sē/] **124–125**
Red Sea [rĕd/ sē/] **124–125**
Sea of Japan [sē/ əv jə păn/] **124–125**
Sea of Okhotsk [sē/ əv ō kätsk/] **124–125**
South Atlantic Ocean [sowth/ ət lăn/tĭk ō/shən] **124–125**
South China Sea [sowth/ chī/nə sē/] **124–125**
Southern Ocean [sŭdh/ərn ō/shən] **124–125**
South Pacific Ocean [sowth/ pə sĭf/ĭk ō/shən] **124–125**

The United States of America
Capital: Washington, D.C. (District Of Columbia)
   [wä/shĭng tən dē/sē/, wö/–]

Regions of the United States
Mid-Atlantic States [mĭd/ət lăn/tĭk stāts/] **123–10**
Midwest [mĭd/wĕst/] **123–9**
New England [nōō/ ĭng/glənd] **123–11**
Pacific States [pə sĭf/ĭk stāts/] **123–7**
Rocky Mountain States [räk/ē mown/tn stāts/] **123–8**
South [sowth] **123–13**
Southeast [sowth/ēst/] **123–13**
Southwest [sowth/wĕst/] **123–12**
West Coast [wĕst/ kōst/] **123–7**

Index

Index

Index